.

THOU SHALL NOT PASS

THOU SHALL NOT PASS

The Anatomy of Football's Centre-Half

Leo Moynihan

BLOOMSBURY SPORT

LONDON · OXFORD · NEW YORK · NEW DELHI · SYDNEY

BLOOMSBURY SPORT
Bloomsbury Publishing Plc
50 Bedford Square, London, WC1B 3DP, UK
29 Earlsfort Terrace, Dublin 2, Ireland

BLOOMSBURY, BLOOMSBURY SPORT and the Diana logo are
trademarks of Bloomsbury Publishing Plc

First published in Great Britain 2021

For legal purposes the Acknowledgements on p. 209
constitute an extension of this copyright page

Plate section design by Austin Taylor
All plate section images © Getty Images

A catalogue record for this book is available from the British Library

Library of Congress Cataloguing-in-Publication data has been applied for

ISBN: HB: 978-14729-7291-0; PB: 978-14729-7290-3;
eBook: 978-14729-7292-7

2 4 6 8 10 9 7 5 3 1

Typeset in Adobe Garamond Pro by Deanta Global Publishing Services,
Chennai, India
Printed and bound in Great Britain by CPI Group (UK) Ltd, Croydon CR0 4YY

To find out more about our authors and books visit www.bloomsbury.com
and sign up for our newsletters

To my daughter, Daisy.
The stylish *libero* in our little team.

CONTENTS

INTRODUCTION

'A Bastard of a Job'

Like Charles Dickens' *Great Expectations*, our story begins on the marshes. 'The dark flat wilderness,' is how the great British author describes his scene, but he could be putting ink to paper and describing Hackney Marshes or any other recreation ground in the land that houses footballers, wiping the sleep from their eyes on a Sunday morning and hoping to make distant dreams come fleetingly true. Among them are centre-halves.

Dickens' great novel was first published in 1860, just weeks before Hallam FC first played Sheffield FC, the world's oldest fixture to date, and while he may have given little regard to the niceties of this strange new pastime, his early description of Magwitch, the escaped convict who startles young Pip in the bleak graveyard, could quite easily be a nation's crude version of what a centre-half might look like:

> A fearful man, all in coarse grey, with a great iron on his leg. A man with no hat, and with broken shoes, and with an old rag tied round his head. A man who had been soaked in water, and smothered in mud, and lamed by stones, and cut by flints, and stung by nettles, and torn by briars; who limped, and shivered, and glared and growled; and whose teeth chattered in his head as he seized me by the chin.

That's the thing about centre-halves. They are seen as fearful, perceived as muddied spoilers; cut, stung and torn; glaring and glowering. There to seize pretty young attackers by the chin. But, like Magwitch himself later proves, there is so much more to the subjects of this book than first meets the eye.

Old Trafford, the autumn of 1986. Dressed in a navy suit and maroon tie, Alex Ferguson signs a contract. He is the new manager of Manchester United. His new home was one of the most modern, most envied and most full stadiums in Europe, but the team he inherited struggling in the old First Division needed immediate rebuilding, and having watched them lose 2–0 at Oxford United days after his arrival, the new manager had no doubts where that construction must start.

At centre-half that afternoon at the Manor Ground, Ferguson played Graeme Hogg and Kevin Moran (Paul McGrath played in midfield). John Aldridge scored a penalty, a Welshman called Neil Slatter got the other and Ferguson left Oxford educated. For he now had knowledge. Those being asked to play in the centre of the team's defence just weren't up to it.

Ferguson had got the job on the back of his incredible success at Aberdeen, a provincial club who, under his stringent stewardship, took on and beat giants at home and across the water. Aberdeen were a brilliant attacking unit, with Gordon Strachan and Mark McGhee among its offensive options, but it was the centre-half pairing of Willie Miller and Alex McLeish that afforded him the solidity he so craved. In 1945, Matt Busby had found a club reduced to rubble by war and in need of concrete as well as footballing nous. Over forty years later, Ferguson found the centre of his new team's defence in need of equal attention.

INTRODUCTION

'Centre-backs were the foundation of my Manchester United sides,' Ferguson has said. 'Always centre-backs. I looked for stability and consistency. Take Steve Bruce and Gary Pallister; until I found those two we were without a prayer. Paul McGrath was constantly injured, Kevin Moran always had split heads. He was like a punch-drunk boxer by the time I became his manager … Graeme Hogg, meanwhile, had not reached the standard we required. So I always told my chairman, "We need centre-backs who will play every week. They give you the steadiness and consistency and continuity."'

To those who like their football sexed up, Ferguson's description might sound a little bland. Steady, consistent, continuous. Good centre-halves can sound like the family car. But, take a closer look and these columns standing steadfast have long contributed so much to the game's ability to enthral. Big, brutish and stubborn, those purists trying too hard to push football as the beautiful game might see our protagonists as the unsightly zit on its nose, but don't be fooled. Centre-halves, in whatever shape or size they come, have always added to both the raw drama of a game, and in their own way, its blinding fun. As Ferguson points out, greatness stems from them – *'Always centre-backs.'*

In May, 1989, Arsenal went to Anfield needing to beat Liverpool by two goals to clinch the First Division title. Their manager, George Graham, a football man with a fondness for the art of central defending, selected three of them. His team needed goals, but he picked three centre-halves, stifled the game and famously won 2–0. At the heart of the defence, Tony Adams and Steve Bould had been a fixture in Arsenal's push for greatness, but that night they were joined by the wily old David O'Leary. The Irishman's presence alongside the other two contained Liverpool's forward line, and throughout the game, O'Leary could be heard shouting, 'I'm taking my two Dobermans for a walk.'

Tony Adams liked that, a lot. No doubt Steve Bould did too. Centre-halves, you see, are a proud breed. The centre-half is playing the game but he is also observing it. Square on, they have the action in front of them, and they act. They wait for danger, prepare for it and guard against it. They must do all they can to keep other, presumably more talented opponents at bay, while also organising, cajoling, lecturing, barking.

Over the years, from the Camp Nou to those Hackney Marshes, preconceptions and stereotypes have man marked these man markers. They are the big brutes, leadened by their lack of ambition, mere ogres hell-bent on killing joy. Some of it is true but there is so much more to these misunderstood souls and today they can be celebrated.

The fact that Liverpool's Dutch maestro, Virgil van Dijk, stood on the shoulder of Lionel Messi at the 2019 Ballon d'Or award ceremony, a gong that many pundits felt he deserved to win, says much for a changing position and for those who had hitherto judged it. Elite coaches such as Pep Guardiola and Jürgen Klopp put their centre-halves at the very core of how they want to play the game. High-tempo, possession football that starts in their own defensive areas with centre-halves who *must* be able to play.

If football under Guardiola is like a swan, his central defenders are the legs under the surface. Mikel Arteta, Guardiola's one-time assistant at Manchester City, remarked while there that, 'Our defenders have to play the ball out … defend well, maintain our offside line, anticipate … know who's pressing you and where the gaps are. After a mistake, you've got to do the difficult thing again – no hiding.' Txiki Begirstain, his director of football at both Barcelona and Manchester, was a little more succinct: 'It is,' he said, 'a bastard of a job'.

And it's not just Pep. Those asked to fill the berth at Marcelo Bielsa's Leeds United might just agree; after all, theirs is a coach who asks them to man-mark strikers, to run, to work. Defending under these thinkers of the game is not only required when under attack, it is for the whole ninety minutes. A bastard of a job.

Dion Dublin, a fine centre-forward who could seamlessly change to a centre-half, using his instincts as the former to aid his time as the latter (so much so that Wayne Rooney, after one game playing against him, commented that he was, in fact, the best central defender he had ever faced). 'I would think like a forward and when I faced Wazza [Rooney], I knew I didn't have his pace, so I thought like him. I read where the ball should go, where I'd want the ball to be if I was the striker, and I got all my decisions right and he got no space at all.'

Today, Dublin sees the role as being more cultured, but agrees that the position of centre-half is as hard as ever. Yes, the fight between the defender and attacker is less of a bare-knuckle affair, but coaches and managers are demanding just as much blood, sweat and tears. 'The object of a centre-half is still the same,' he says. 'You have to stop the opposition from scoring, and to do that you still have to be a bit horrible. Destroy before you create. Today they are being asked to start things and play, which can be nice to watch, but lose it back there, you risk everything. It is undoubtably the [most] demanding position in the modern game. At the very top, they must have everything.'

Virgil van Dijk at Liverpool certainly represents that everything. A centre-half, yes, there to prevent his team's agony, but still very much part of its ecstasy. 'I feel as big a part of the team as anyone,' he told me. 'Everyone wants to see exciting things on the pitch; goals, nutmegs, tricks, but just because I am a central defender, I still feel important and valuable. I never feel like my team or the game doesn't need me. I feel the importance of my role and my position.'

This book wants to get into the muddy penalty area and examine what makes the centre-half tick. They are an enigmatic bunch. Hard, but emotional. None came as hard or as emotional as Terry Butcher. A player made iconic by literally spilling his blood for his country, he became notably moved when asked, for this book, to place himself back in time, on an unfamiliar field of play, his team winning by a single goal, the game approaching its end, the crowd baying for his and his team's blood, demanding their goal, and it is his and his defensive companions' job to stop them. 'Thou shall not pass,' came his war cry. Yes, he is advocating and celebrating the prevention of what we all want – a goal – but there lies the beauty. It is his beauty. His job.

These pages will take a look at how that job has changed tactically. From the original midfield playmaker, then asked to retreat, the centre-half eventually became the centre-back, but not necessarily by everyone. Some purists will argue about how we should label them, but in this book, we will call them centre-halves. Apologies if that offends.

By talking to the likes of Butcher and Tony Adams, we'll ask why centre-halves have long made for great captains. Do they rule by fear (are they really all Dobermans?) or is theirs the gift of insight?

And what of their weapons? One chapter examines the art of the defensive header. A niche subject if ever there was one, but when Darren Moore – a centre-half who towers over the gigantic category – spoke with very real passion on the subject, you could have been talking to Arnold Palmer about the perfect drive from the first tee. All timing and skill, compounded by years of practice.

Then there are their sharper weapons. Those that hurt. The dark arts have long been used to quell a pesky forward's tide, and here we will examine how a trained elbow, a hardened skull and some sharpened studs were a necessity, come Saturday afternoon's frivolities. 'Kenneth, the number 10 …' Brian Clough could be heard shouting at his Nottingham Forest centre-half, Kenny Burns, prior to kick-off: '… No shin pads.' Burns explains here that he knew exactly what his boss meant, and would act accordingly.

This book will also look at the great central defensive partnerships, just as vital as your attacking variety and perhaps more nuanced. Talking of relationships, what of the centre-halves' rapport with their goalkeepers, and with the centre-forward they are paid to keep quiet? Both are scrutinised here and both prove as fractious as the other.

But there is also beauty here. The artisans among any list of central defenders have long been admired and are celebrated. The ball-playing central defender is a curious breed. Don't be fooled that they are new to our game. In the 1960s and 1970s, green shoots sprouted from the muddiest of pitches. Bobby Moore, of course, is a symbol of 1960s Cool Britannia and moving forward, players such as Tony Adams, for too long ridiculed for his team's desire to defend with a capital D, emerged as the finest of footballers when the ball was at his feet.

Mark Lawrenson, Liverpool's ball-playing centre-half in the 1980s, talked to me about his international days with the

Republic of Ireland under Jack Charlton. On getting the job and meeting his players, Charlton, himself a fine filler of the centre-half berth, made his feelings clear. The abilities that Lawrenson had – more than comfortable with the ball, a desire to pass and create – these weren't meant for Charlton's new backline. 'You're not playing at the back for me,' Charlton said in no uncertain terms. 'You're a midfielder.'

While forwards are designed to get bums off seats, asked to get the heart racing, centre-halves are required to keep bums on seats, to slow the heart; but still they are complex, misunderstood, too often pigeonholed. Yes, football's centre-halves are in fact a most vibrant stitch in the game's rich tapestry. This is their story.

1

FIX BAYONETS, LADS!

A Celebration of the Art of Defending

The World Cup held in Italy in 1990 offered the fan a smorgasbord of iconic moments. Cameroon's early win over Argentina amid some agricultural tackling, Salvatore Schillaci's piercing hitman eyes that carried a host nation's hopes within them, Frank Rijkaard letting Rudi Völler's face become acquainted with what he had for lunch. For the English there was Gazza's tears, and a David Platt swivel; even Gary Lineker letting his lunch out in differing ways to Rijkaard is an image that has lasted the tests of time.

So, what of our centre-halves? Quietly it was a World Cup that England stepped from the 4-4-2 shadows, bringing a sense of Continental chic to the position. Suddenly, to Terry and Derek from Aldershot on the terraces, the word *sweeper* meant more than an instrument in their old dear's broom cupboard.

But, while the tactical flexibility shown by Messrs Terry Butcher, Mark Wright and Des Walker gave the whole team a dimension hitherto unseen, their sheer Englishness could never be fully extinguished.

'Take Des Walker,' says Chris Waddle, a major part of that England side's creativity. 'Des was a brilliant player. Not the biggest, but he was quick and he could play. The thing is, we had to convince him to play a bit more. Des loved to defend. That's great, but at the highest level of international football I for one felt like we needed more. "Des," I'd say. "Des, play a bit more. You're a really good player."

'He looked at me and he said, "I'm paid to fucking defend. I'm not paid to look good."'

And there we have it. 'You'll never beat Des Walker' was the chant doing the rounds at the time, and no doubt music to its subject's ears, such was his attitude about his craft, an attitude deep-set in centre-halves for so very long. An attitude vital to it, for stopping goals had to be the key.

The modern game is obsessed with aesthetics. New stadiums, immaculate pitches, the blind hope that VAR will bring perfection to its officiating. Centre-halves today must be able to start attacks, they must join in. Centre-halves are handsome, dominating, able to command the largest of fees and wages, but only if they can play.

But what of the reason they are really there? 'A rock at the back' was how central defenders used to be described. Now, shinier and prettier than ever before, they are more like sticks of rock found at the seaside, sweet, but surely running through them must be that priority – *I'm paid to fucking defend.*'

Has the game forgotten to appreciate nuts-and-bolts defending, and the players who enjoy throwing themselves in the way of those handsome attackers? Is there even a place for such ugliness? The player who actually enjoys throwing water on the flames of creativity: is he a thing of the past?

A centre-half with his broken nose and scarred brow has today become almost unwanted; like Frankenstein's monster, desperate to be loved but instead reviled, given up as cumbersome and slow-witted. Even those who excel at their work are seen as somehow from the old school and the days when a centre-half was simply known as 'the stopper'.

In his book, *The Soccer Syndrome*, John Moynihan spoke fondly of watching the post-war game and those big brutes at the back. 'The good old stopper in a WM formation was supposed to stay put with eyes feasting on the rival centre-forward like a casino manager watching a con man,' he wrote. 'I can still hear the tackles meted out on number 9s by Jack Chisholm of Brentford, Allenby Chilton (Manchester United) and Frank Brennan (Newcastle). Good, strong, solid, tackling; biff, bang, crunch to make a centre-forward know he was in a game.'

You won't find much in the way of biff, bang or crunch on modern coaching courses, but is that to the detriment of the position and the game? There must be room for those who relish being the last line. Those hearty souls who as the pressure grows, inflate with it, and who think nothing of placing their face between the football and its destination.

Snobbish attitudes prevail in a game where some feel that the centre-half must simply receive the ball and pass the ball, they must start pretty patterns of play; their defensive duties be damned. For all that, you will still find players who put high stock in doing a team's dirty work, seeing it as a potent weapon in his arsenal, and who's out-and-out infatuation with preventing goals must match any striker's fondness for scoring them.

Kenny Burns – a sometime goalscorer at Birmingham at the start of his career, but centre-half in Brian Clough's great Nottingham Forest team that won back-to-back European Cups in 1979 and 1980 – had such a fondness and in his no-nonsense Glaswegian tones, can hardly hide his enthusiasm for defending.

'The goalscorers got the headlines but playing well at the back and stopping them scoring, I thought it was as good as a goal. I can't do what John Robertson could do. I can't do what Trevor Francis could do. My skill set was different so get on with it. Trevor was getting all the headlines, but if I played and we won to nothing, I was more than happy.'

There are modern-day centre-halves who wholeheartedly agree. 'It's your job,' says Shane Duffy, the Republic of Ireland's dominating centre-half. 'I think it's a dying art. The game has developed, but the game's basics remain. I have to defend my goal and it's a great feeling when you are doing just that. Keeping a clean sheet is far better for me than scoring a goal.

'There are some defenders out there who like to defend but it isn't their main priority. That seems mad to me. Just playing and enjoying playing isn't enough. I think you need a streak through you that wants more than just fun.'

It's an attitude that would bring a smile to the granite-like face of the Juventus centre-half, Giorgio Chiellini, a name who draws gasps of appreciation from most centre-halves who share his almost biblical desire to prevent footballs meeting the netting.

In the spring of 2018, the Italian played against Tottenham in the Champions League with his side's progress at the end of the tie dependent on his determination to close down space, block goal-bound efforts and get any part of his body in the way of the English side's efforts. It was a performance that had Jamie Carragher, the former Liverpool and England centre-half, drooling on his couch as he watched an individual performance that he says, 'Made me jump out of my seat and applaud the television set.'

Let's take the 2005 and 2012 Champions League finals. Two nights that are forever etched in English football history, two nights when millions of backsides left seats, two nights when millions of television sets garnered applause. The latter, in Munich, saw Chelsea claim victory. While the glory-hunting minds-eye will always see Didier Drogba's late leap and winning penalty, read the game's small-print and it is clear that it was the back four, the goalkeeper, and David Luiz alongside Gary Cahill at centre-half whose total reluctance to be bamboozled by Bavarian bombardments won the night, and ensured that the famous old trophy would reside with a London postcode for the first time.

And then there is Istanbul. The 2005 Champions League campaign will be, for generations to come, talked about using terms such as *miracle* and *my God, did that really happen?*, but look beyond the sheer utter madness of Liverpool's comeback and it is Carragher's total objection to AC Milan retaking the lead that has everything to do with the eventual win. The socks rolled around his calves, the veins on show throbbing with cramp. Block after block and pain-ridden stretches to frustrate the Italian frontline spoke of a footballer programmed to shut out opposing glory.

'When I played, my thing every game – like a striker thinks only of scoring – was keeping a clean sheet,' he says. 'That was everything to me. If you got a clean sheet, no matter how I had played, that was my job done. On another day I might play really well, but if we had conceded goals, that wasn't right. My job was to stop goals, my job was to keep clean sheets and as a club, we were big on that.

'I'd be obsessed about it. I'd study the goals against columns in the league table as much as I did our position. Under Gérard Houllier and then Rafa Benítez it was a massive thing.

'Pepe Reina would often win the Golden Glove trophy for clean sheets, which made me laugh because most of the time he had nothing to do. And he gets the trophy?! Sami Hyypiä and me always wondered what that was all about.'

It is a blinkered view of the game that some players, perhaps themselves preoccupied with what they see as the more beautiful side of football, find hard to fathom. At the World Cup in 1990, John Barnes, England's dynamic forward, talked about the aesthetics of a goal and admitted that he couldn't understand the mindset of someone like his teammate Terry Butcher, who seemed so fond of stopping one.

'I used to say, "Clean sheets, no defeats",' Butcher says. 'It was an obsession to me. It was the work you put in to get it, too. I used to love it. That was the high. You'd blocked, tackled, even winning the first header and getting on top of the centre-forward, that was the big thrill. It's destroying, rather than creating. I loved that.'

There's that word again, *obsession*. It seems particular personality traits are on show here. 'Growing up, I was very into organising,' Butcher says. 'I actually started playing in goal and got told off for shouting too much. I had every defensive attitude and a very defensive mentality. I also enjoyed kicking people.'

The last point may raise the odd grimace, but bruises aside, a centre-half will talk to you with a definite and natural glint in the eye when it comes to doing his work, and that goes for any level of the game. Ben Martin has played for several non-league clubs, but even at 6 foot 7, he agrees that it is personality rather than sheer brawn that aids the footballer.

'You have to have a different character and mentality,' he says. 'I think we are different types of people. In my general life, I am very stubborn. I'm organised, I like to lead. Basically I'm a bit of a control freak.'

At Wimbledon in the 1980s and 1990s, anything that upset the aesthetics was greeted with relish. Alan Reeves, the club's centre-half in the mid-1990s, loved facing down seemingly superior football teams and making sure their route to goal was never an easy one. 'You have to enjoy it,' he says. 'As a centre-half, that's your primary purpose, getting the ball out of the danger area. Stopping goals. Everything else is a bonus.

'I loved backs against the wall stuff. Nine times out of ten, we were the second best on paper, so your back against the wall was the usual. We had each other's backs though and loved it. That's why we got so many good results. We drowned teams. It was trenches football every week.

'We'd work on it in training and it was as intense as it would be on match day. I loved those attack versus defence sessions. Nine versus six. Nine attackers against six of us defenders. Bring it on! These c***s aren't scoring against us.'

Controlling a game may be perceived as the job of the fine central midfielder, whose ability to keep the ball dictates pace but control to these centre-halves is about organising, barking orders, controlling a game when the opposition have the upper hand, and it is these games that stay in their memory.

Darren Moore, formerly of West Bromwich Albion, was the sort of centre-half you might see from space. Press him on his career memories and he'll take you back to one satisfying afternoon. 'I've played in matches that won promotions and games that I've scored important goals, but when I look back on my playing days, I take myself to Highbury in 2004,' he says. 'We were playing against that Invincibles team. Vieira, Henry, Pires. That lot.

'They were 1–0 up but with ten minutes left, we equalised and then, well goodness me, we were up against it. It was tough, the crowd are roaring them on, but you do your job. It's tough but you leave with a point. The ball is coming in the box and you're getting things on it. Two things are happening. You are concentrating on your own positional sense but you are also organising others around you.

'What I liked in those moments is all your teammates are looking to you to guide them through the rest of the game. You feel your teammates are looking at you to be a pillar of strength at their time of need. That's when it's great. People ask me my favourite game, and that's the one.'

A former striker can lie back and picture a match-winning goal; a midfielder, a piercing through-ball; and a goalkeeper, an acrobatic save; but talk to many centre-halves and their happy place is a wall, and their backs are firmly against it. 'If I could go back to playing in my mind, it is always those matches, those last twenty minutes, holding on to a lead, and you're under the cosh,' says Carragher, as if reminiscing about an old holiday romance.

'We went to some hard places and kept clean sheets. Barcelona three times and we only conceded one goal. We went to the Bernabéu, we went to the San Siro, we went to Juventus, and never conceded. That was down to hard bloody work, especially mentally. I look back at those times, and miss them.

'They were special nights. Hanging on, playing against brilliant strikers, organising, shouting, tackling, blocking, getting my head on things, it was brilliant. In Europe especially, it was all about huge mental concentration. You'd fall into your bed, exhausted, on those nights. It wasn't because you'd done that much running but the fatigue came from the mental work you had done to ensure that clean sheet. You knew that if you switched off for one second, you were in trouble. I loved it. There has to be a place for that though because that's the game. Teams, however good they are, will be under the cosh and a centre-half has got to be able to handle that.'

Handling is one thing; clearly totally thriving on it is another, and to hear Terry Butcher talk about a hypothetical match you understand the difference. 'Let's say my team are one up at Old Trafford,' he says. 'There's ten minutes left and they are coming at you, desperate for an equaliser. The crowd is getting behind them and your win is on the line. Those are the great times. I used to shout to my back four, "Fix bayonets, lads!"'

Bayonets, digging in, being in the trenches; there is a certain militaristic tilt that occurs when discussing defending in this country, but what is it really like when the bombs are dropping? What makes some centre-halves so reluctant to raise the white flag? 'There is no worse feeling than conceding a goal,' says Ben Martin. 'When the ball is coming over and you sense the danger, the striker has half a yard and thinks he has it and you react, nick in and take the ball away from him, that's the moment.'

Carragher can easily take himself back into a busy penalty area and argues that last-gasp defending is as much a skill as dribbling and scoring. 'Sometimes, things just slow down,' he says. 'There mustn't be panic despite what is happening around you. There is a last-gasp tackle to be made, and you know that you can make it. It should happen very calmly, although it doesn't look like that. If you rush it, you can dive in too early. You often see a striker's shot go through the defender's legs, and that's because the tackle has been rushed and you have gone too early.

You have to time it. The striker hasn't pulled his foot back. You gauge the situation, you sense the danger, you time the challenge.'

Shane Duffy sees the work he does in the box as merely his natural game. 'I'm not the quickest but you learn to sense danger,' he says. 'It might seem simple to someone watching in the stand, but I am constantly thinking about the game around me, constantly thinking about possible dangers. Hopefully you can quell danger by reading the play well, but you can't always get it right. Sometimes you get it wrong, and you have to throw your head at it. You have to be brave.'

Bravery. That quality demanded of centre-halves and summed up perhaps most potently by the image of Terry Butcher walking from a Swedish football pitch in 1989, a slightly manic look in his eye, his bandaged head still pumping blood all over his England shirt.

When it comes to brave defending, Butcher's bloodied face is only a small part of it. Today, bravery is often a term used to describe the modern centre-halves' desire to get on the ball, to take possession in the tightest of situations, but it is also a word Harry Redknapp is quick to pin on his old mate, Bobby Moore, a defender (arguably England's greatest) usually thought of only in terms of the more decorative side of the game.

'Bobby was so brave,' Redknapp says. 'The country love how stylish a footballer Bobby was, but he would do the rough stuff. You don't see much of it now, but Bobby would put his head in where it hurts. The thing is, it wasn't often that he'd have to as he was so good at reading the game and its dangers. We'd always laugh at West Ham that Bobby never came off the pitch muddy. This wasn't because he didn't enjoy a last-gasp block or tackle, but he could steal the ball so cleverly. He was though as brave as he was good.'

One iconic example of Moore's own kind of bravery came in Mexico during the 1970 World Cup. England, the World Champions and many people's favourites, were facing Brazil, just as many people's favourites. A group game played in searing heat, Brazil were showing the class that would take them to the title, and in a brilliant, tense game, their winger, Jairzinho, broke free in midfield and started to run at England's penalty area. Here was a player who that month would tie knots around the world, and between him and the goal was only Bobby Moore.

Moore backs off, and backs off. This is brave defending even without the broken noses and cut heads. A forward on top of his game, intent on beating you, but you wait, you bide your time; the impulse is to attack the player, to lunge at him, but he waits, and then there it is. Moore, like an elegant heron patiently awaiting its fishy lunch, takes the ball from Jairzinho's eager feet and calmly, the ball is played forward. The most beautiful piece of 'ugly' defending you'll ever see.

Beauty? Some will scoff but while Terry Butcher may try to explain himself to non-believers by saying he is a destroyer rather than a creator, he would agree with many who see so much skill in what he and others must do. Now that Darren Moore is a coach and his employment depends on what his centre-halves do, he further appreciates his former position.

'Done well, it is an art,' he says. 'It's an ability to be in the position and to deal with danger. Look at Cristiano Ronaldo in his opponent's penalty box. He is so composed. He sees the moment. He knows the moment. He has been there so many times, and so he can relax and score. Class defending is the same. You have an ability to spot danger early and you assess it and within a millisecond, you can position yourself, make the right choices and make that block.

'Look at the likes of Giorgio Chiellini at Juventus. He has that skill, he has that art. When you start stripping back the game, and looking at what players like Chiellini do and what Carragher did at Liverpool, it's fascinating because this isn't mindless stuff, pure bravery or doggedness, this is an art and these guys are assessing the play, making the right decisions and stopping goals.

'I can try to coach it and I do, but so much comes with experience. Experience buys that calmness, that ability to focus on the danger. You gain the ability to remain calm. Balls can be coming in the box and it doesn't even have to be a brave lunge or block, great last-gasp defending can be just stepping across the striker's line and preventing any danger. You haven't headed the ball but nor has the striker, now that's good defending. These players have trained eyes and play with them.'

But what of the modern game and its future centre-halves? Are trained eyes, stoic minds and brave hearts being ignored in favour of clever feet? 'I think we might lose the last-gasp, brave defender who will do anything he can to stop a goal,' says Carragher. 'I'm not saying that is totally bad, as the game is full of brilliant centre-halves, brilliant on the ball, but it's evolving and if top coaches want to play a certain way, then players who want to play at the top level are going to have to be that type of defender.

'People are looking at their passing, how they are stepping into midfield, how are they contributing to their side's offensive movements. The top-level lads are not judged purely on how they stop attacks.'

Terry Butcher takes it even further, painting a picture of what he sees as the modern-day centre-half: 'He has big bushy hair, an earring, tattoos, pink football boots, he's wearing undergarments, long shorts, cycling shorts under the long shorts. That would never have happened in my day. Centre-halves should always be the rock upon which good teams are built.'

He may sound like a tipsy uncle at Christmas, deriding the quality of the day's television stars, but is Butcher merely underlining Carragher's point that today's players need not be so robust? Shane Duffy, his arm covered in tattoos and his feet dressed in brightly coloured boots, smiles when he hears the quote, his competitive streak finely tuned on Ireland's Gaelic football pitches firmly pricked.

'Butcher is a legend,' he says. 'What he doesn't know is that we wear the boots that they send us. I might wear pink boots but I stick my head in where it hurts! I know where my strengths lie and I just want to prove what I am good at. I'm not a ball-playing centre-half, and won't play ten through balls in a match. I concentrate on my game.'

And even a player lauded as the complete modern centre-half appreciates all aspects of life in the position, whether that be the aesthetic side of the game or the more agricultural. Virgil van Dijk and last gasp, back-to-the-wall defending don't seem like obvious bedfellows, but he rejects the notion that his modern brethren don't embrace it.

'I think it happens to us quite a lot,' he says. 'Look at the 2019 Champions League final. We can be a goal up and the opponent is trying to do everything possible to try and win the game. We had our backs against the wall in Madrid against Tottenham, and yes, it is a different situation to what we normally have, because yes, we are usually attacking and pressing forward, but there are times when we have to drop and we have to organise, and you must take joy in that part of the game.

'You want to push forward, lose the ball high, but win it high too, and be on the front foot. I want to come off the pitch sort of thinking I can play again. That would be the perfect game, because it would mean we've all been perfect, we've all done our job; but I am definitely taking enjoyment from those harder moments.

'That season, in the group stages, we played Napoli needing to win. We were 1–0 up and really under pressure at the end, but Allison made that sick save, knowing "One goal, we are out". When Allison made that save, I went to him and celebrated with him like he had scored! It feels so important and helped us win the Champions League. I enjoy both sides. I prefer to be comfortable though. That's just me, maybe.

'Look at the semi-final second-leg against Barcelona. Three goals down but then four up, knowing one goal, and we were out. It was incredible to keep a clean sheet that night against Lionel Messi, an individual whom I think is the best to ever play the game. We did it that night though.'

Steph Houghton, centre-half at Manchester City and England, is playing highly technical, press-beating, high-risk football with the ball at her feet, but she agrees that she must be prepared to put in the dirty work. Not just prepared. She must relish it: 'There's nothing better than winning your first contact, whether that's on the ground or in the air,' she says. 'That's as good as a goal to me. The way I have been brought up and the way I have been coached is all about doing your job and a lot of that is about winning your tackles, making your blocks. It breeds confidence. I know that if I am winning those challenges, if I am dominating physically, and winning my one-on-one battles, then my whole game improves.'

Whether you're Houghton at Manchester City, van Dijk in a Champions League final or Shane Duffy in a Premier League scrap, centre-halves are being asked to be multifaceted, and more and more, must be able to do it all. Whereas those hearty stoppers of the post-war game were there to purely stop while the game went on around them, today's ancestors must be involved.

'Every single player is being asked to be involved with the game,' Darren Moore says. 'If you look at the position now, centre-halves are a different build and a different structure. Strikers are a different build and a different structure. With these different shapes and different tactics there is a chance that the game loses its out-and-out defenders. The game has turned, academies are coaching players differently. Football is very possession based and if a team dominates the possession, defending isn't required as much.'

But hold on, isn't that a depressing way to end the conversation? There has always been a love of the last-gasp block, the kind of play that just as a supporter fears the horror of a goal, a player slides in and like the state governor phoning death row, offers a reprieve. Moore smiles and offers a knowing laugh. Surely his career choice depends on such moments? 'You can't ignore the so-called ugly side of the game and a team must be good without the ball. If you have a centre-half who has that doggedness too, I tell you what, you have a good chance of winning a football match.'

2

STOPPERS AND
STARTERS

The Tactical Changes at Centre-Half

E. A. Cross, or Edwin to his mother, strolled nonchalantly from the pavilion dressing rooms to the pitch. His Wrexham side are about to take on their arch-rivals Druids in the inaugural Welsh Cup final. Edwin, a clerk at a local insurance company, was at ease. An early spring breeze on his face will have pleased him, reminding him that the cricket (his true passion) season will soon begin and he will replace his newly invented shin pads with the more comfortable batting equivalent that he enthusiastically wears playing for the Wrexham Cricket Club.

He had only taken up football, that more gruff sport to fill the winter months and to keep fit, but here he is about to play in his country's cup final and while he yearned to hear leather on willow, this is serious and he has tactical instructions to follow.

The bumper crowd is focused. It's 1878. The cup competition may be new but the distaste each club has for the other has been cemented in recent times. Benjamin Disraeli, the prime minister, may have mobilised reserves in anticipation of war with Russia the day before, and in America, Thomas Edison might have recently patented his phonograph, but here in this corner of north Wales, battles and music can wait.

Wrexham's captain and full-back, Charles Murless, had made a change to his team. Edwin, so often deployed in a packed forward line, will play a deeper role, the pace of the centre-forward, John Price, deemed sufficient. Instead, Edwin will play as a centre-half and Wrexham will win the game 1–0.

That night, while Edwin will have wistfully dreamt of his cricket whites, local estate agent Murless might well have proudly sipped on his evening pint of Welsh beer, but for all his tactical nous, he could not have boasted of having invented what would be called 'the centre-half'. Edwin, playing as the centre with two half-backs and making a 2-3-5 formation, or pyramid, wasn't entirely new, but it was novel, and the fact that they managed to stem the Druids' 2-2-6 tide, spoke volumes of a new way of playing the game, a defter way, perhaps more defensive, but certainly more subtle and less gung-ho.

Many have speculated about who first laid the foundation bricks of football's innovative pyramid system. The Hungarian coach Árpád Csanádi wrote in his coaching manual, *Soccer*, that it was Cambridge United in 1883, who first deployed the centre-half in a 2-3-5. E. A. Cross' efforts five years earlier prove that theory redundant, and Jonathan Wilson in his excellent book, *Inverting the Pyramid*, points out that Nottingham Forest in the late 1870s were also utilising it. Taking one forward from a packed line up front gave additional cover, but also lent itself to a game trying to move away from its brutish origins.

With change comes ridicule. In 1882, the *Scottish Athletic Journal* bemoaned this new-fangled idea that not every player needed to attack, when it wrote that two players rigidly staying back were there only to 'keep the goalkeeper in chat'. As football progressed, the relationship between centre-halves and goal-keepers would become both fractious and vital. The image of idle chat is an amusing one, but the writer's contemptuous tone did suggest that plenty of observers wanted to see a forward-centric game, whereas defenders were mere cannon fodder, offering little to any actual enjoyment of proceedings and certainly not to any tactical conversations.

In time, that would change. The centre-half would become a kingpin in the 2-3-5 pyramid formation that so dominated the game for the early part of the twentieth century. Tactical explorers such as Herbert Chapman would change things further with his three-back formation, making stoppers of our protagonists, before partnerships, sweepers, hackers and cultured types would make the position such a varied corner of football's tactical tapestry.

In keeping with the bruising image that football's centre-half would garner over the years, the origins of football were very much about brute strength. For so long, football had been about the mob. In 1717, the *Stamford Mercury* wrote a piece bemoaning the activities of those outside of the gentry:

'On Monday last the commons gave leave to bring in a bill to prevent the mischiefs which frequently happen by throwing at cocks, and kicking footballs within the city of London and Westminster, and bills of morality.'

Ah yes, morality. If football at the start of George I's reign was seen as akin to cock fighting, then those with the best interests of the country at heart would strive to take action and save people from themselves. Parliamentary bills were passed to attempt to stop this violent pastime, especially in and around London, where the country's wealthy resided, and wanted to do so without fear of a football match sullying their day.

And it wasn't only London. In 1746, an article warning of an upcoming game in the *Derby Mercury* spoke of ensuing trouble and severe circumstances. Who knows what Dave Mackay (who would stand rock-like in Derby's central defence over two hundred years later) would have made of it?

It having been represented to the MAGISTRATES of this Borough, that on Shrove-Tuesday, which will be the third day of March next, there will be a public FOOTBALL-PLAYING in the said Borough; and that such has been lately notified and proclaimed in towns and counties adjacent to the Borough aforesaid, by some person or persons disposed to be at the Head of Tumults and Disorders. These are to give Notice, that Mr MAYOR, and Others His Majesty's Justices of the Peace for the said Borough, do direct and order, that no riotous or tumultuous meeting of any persons, (and more, typically of foreigners at this unhappy Time of contagion amongst horned cattle) do appear at the time and for the purpose aforesaid in the said Borough, on Pain of being rigorously prosecuted for the same, as well as for the consequences of breaking windows, and doing other Mischiefs to the persons and properties of the inhabitants of this borough.

Fast forward eighty years, though, and the same paper has shredded its judgemental tone and celebrates a recent game, underlining the fact that the game was being accepted among the more chattering of classes. In 1827, the *Derby Mercury* wrote the following: 'This annual diversion was on Tuesday last exhibited in our streets with its wonted spirit. How the practice originated is impossible to trace … no public amusement is calculated to call forth such a high degree of public excitement.' Like a character in one of Jane Austen's novels so popular at the time, it seemed that football was climbing social ladders.

It was the desire for a widespread Christian masculinity – good decent young men diverted from life's more carnal desires – that brought the game into the supposed upper echelons of a now Victorian Britain. In 1848, Cambridge United wrote a set of rules for other universities to follow, rules that still allowed for the handling of the ball and character building bust-ups.

Fifteen years later, the newly formed Football Association made their mark on the game and its fledgling rules gave birth to association football. However, it was the Scots in 1872, brushing a layer of sophistication onto the game and giving it a more polished look with cerebral passes and derring-do dribbling offering a less punchy vibe that took the game from Victorian mayhem to Edwardian refinement.

The first 'proper' international played between Scotland and England, at the West of Scotland cricket ground at Hamilton Crescent in Partick, saw the teams play out a goalless draw. Strange, as the hosts played a 2-2-6 formation against England's 1-2-7. Reports told of two packed goalmouths, plenty of action, but no goals. *Bell's Life* went as far as to say the match was, 'one of the jolliest, one of the most spirited and most pleasant matches that have ever been played'.

This was football without tactics. England's lone defender was Harwood Greenhalgh, the Notts County full-back, but very much in the rugby sense of the term, and often aided in his defending by his goalkeeper. England's team that day was a stone heavier per man, but Scotland's new way of playing with their minds as well as their bodies was the standout feature of a wet afternoon and with it, football had gained some sort of philosophy.

And what of our centre-halves? E. A. Cross and Sam Woodison would make their mark, but as the 2-3-5 pyramid formation took hold and mapped out the game moving towards the twentieth century, the position became key, especially in England. Ability was what mattered. When Scotland adopted the centre-half role in 1887, some onlookers felt they had lost some of their attacking prowess, but a piece in the *Scottish Referee* in 1889 argued otherwise, singling out Celtic's James Kelly as an example of the advantages of the position when filled by a quality footballer. 'There are many people who believe that when Scotland adopted the centre-half-back position she sacrificed much of her power in the game,' it read. 'We do not share altogether this opinion, and if players who fill this space in our clubs were men of Mr Kelly's calibre there would be no difference of opinion on the matter, nor would we have any cause to regret having followed England in this matter.'

James Kelly was typical of the new position. A catalyst in the team, both defensively and in attack, the centre-half was becoming the spot that called for the best. Kelly, a Catholic from an Irish background, was taken by Celtic, a new club in Glasgow's East End, from Renton, causing an uproar in West Dunbartonshire, so much so that fans began to sing sectarian songs and called for a ban on signing Catholic players as it was obvious they would only want to eventually join this new powerful club called Celtic.

Kelly was an instant star at Celtic: their first captain, a scorer in their first game (made better by it being a 5–2 win over

Rangers), winning the club's first honours and becoming *the* star of a fledging institution. Kelly's game was no-nonsense. Blessed with pace, and commanding in the air, he could repel attacks, but with the ball, he was no-nonsense, and the key was his ability to quickly switch defence into attack.

The centre-half-back was very much the conductor. Setting the tone, the pace of a game with ever-growing thoughtful play. In 1907, the Woolwich Arsenal centre-half Percy Sands wrote an article in the *Sheffield Telegraph and Star Sports Special*, asking if 'football was becoming more scientific'. He wrote, 'one hears of the adaptation of various combinations such as the open game, the short passing game, the triangular movement, the kick and rush method, the individual method, and so on'.

That it was a centre-half pointing out these diverse tactical approaches spoke volumes for the position he played and the gravitas that was becoming afforded to his centre-half brethren. Gravitas was exactly what Alex Raisbeck, a hugely impressive figure from Stirlingshire, brought to fill Liverpool's centre-half position in 1898, going on to be the new club's first superstar.

That superstars could come in centre-half form was telling in itself, for this was an era when sportsmen were competing with and even replacing military figures in the hearts of an adoring public. Alex Raisbeck, one of seven brothers, all of whom became soldiers or footballers, epitomised that *Boy's Own* hero.

Raisbeck was a swashbuckler. Well-built, 5 foot 10, but with a leap, blond, moustachioed, he was an Edwardian pin-up boy. At centre-half, he could dominate a game of football, winning aerial battles and preventing attacks, but in a swift act able to get on the ball and play decisive balls upfield, while also chipping in with his share of goals.

If as 2017 turned into 2018, Liverpool manager Jürgen Klopp made it his sole business to sign the Dutch centre-half Virgil van Dijk, his predecessor Tom Watson, Liverpool's secretary and first manager, saw similar traits in Raisbeck and knew this was a player who could make his new club move from good to great.

Two years after signing, Raisbeck was made club captain and he lifted the club's first ever league championship in 1901, and their second in 1906. He was the talk of Merseyside and beyond, the living embodiment of the new centre-half. After a cup tie against Everton at Goodison Park in 1905, one scribe was moved to write:

> Never has Raisbeck shown more wondrous football. He was here, there and everywhere. Now initiating an attack, now breaking up another, and again chasing [Jack] Sharp when that lithe young man appeared to be all on his own. He dominated the whole field, and was, without question, the one superlative player. I am never inclined to over-elaborate praise, but truly, Alec Raisbeck was a giant among pygmies.

In 1924, fifteen years after he left the club, Victor Hall wrote a tribute, saying:

> Raisbeck was wholeheartedly a destroyer of attacks when it came from the opposing wing. We have said that he was speed in turn and on the run. We might amplify this and say, that we have never seen in England, a speedier half-back, who could tackle a speedy forward, turn with him,

and overtake and tackle him again. There may be and may have been others so gifted. We have not seen them. His judgement was sound, his valour outstanding and, naturally for a half-back, his control and placing of the ball was equally confident. During his playing career at Anfield, he had to meet forwards whose names and records were outstanding in the history of the game, and yet of none of them could it be said that they were the superior or master of Raisbeck's defensive play. His temperament rarely failed him, no matter how vigorous the play he had to meet.

The play centre-halves had to meet after the First World War began to be more pronounced, forwards more skilful, more physical, their wingmen more sophisticated and with that, the men building football teams whose aim it was to win trophies, started to think of ways that would nullify them, even if it meant forgoing some of their own attacking ambition.

Herbert Chapman, an honest but limited forward, was managing Huddersfield in the early 1920s, and making them the best in the country – they won three consecutive league titles between 1923 and 1926 – came with an eye on a more robust form of defence. Years before he joined Arsenal and created his WM formation, with the emphasis on a third back or 'stopper' centre-half, Chapman had shown signs of his conservatism when he deployed his centre-half, Tom Wilson, in the 1922 FA Cup final in a far deeper role than usual. Huddersfield won the final, 1–0, a scoreline that would please many stoic centre-halves for decades to come, and Wilson was labelled 'the great spoiler' by a jubilant *Huddersfield Examiner*.

For the start of the 1925/26 season, and now working his magic down south at Arsenal, Chapman, like every manager, had his hand forced by the new offside rule that decreed a player was offside if there were two opponents between him and the goal line, where previously it had been three. Frequent stoppages, constant cries of 'Offside!', the game needed the change and it was an instant success in as much as there was a spike in goalmouth action and goals. For cerebral types such as Chapman though – a manager who specialised in springing constant offside traps under the old rule – who were not in the game to merely entertain, steps needed to be taken and at Arsenal, they quickly were.

It was a 7–0 defeat at Arsenal that made certain that a change needed to come and it was player-power (so often vital if tactical revolution is to be enforced) that helped oil the tactical pistons. Charlie Buchan, a roaring talent in a roaring decade, had been tempted to Highbury from Sunderland for a lot of money and having felt the shame of the seven-goal drubbing at his old rivals on the Tyne, he spoke to Chapman about his frustrations (he called his new employers a 'team without a plan') and underlined the need in the modern game to withdraw your centre-half from midfield dynamo to back three frustraters.

Chapman listened and waited, but needed no lectures in innovation. A student of the game, he would have known that it was a tactic oft used. C. B. Fry, back in 1897, wrote in the *Encyclopaedia of Sport and Games* of using the player in purely defensive terms:

Sometimes, when a side is a goal or two ahead, and it is thought advisable to play a purely defensive game, a third-back is added by diminishing the number of forwards …

with regard to the shift of withdrawing a forward and putting an extra back, there is much to be said: that the three backs are extremely hard to get through ... but unless the players thus moved are versatile and capable of performing satisfactorily the duties of their altered positions ... it is certainly unwise to play a third back, unless the extra man is a capable player in that position.

Chapman wanted capable players and at Arsenal, he had them. Yes, there was the new offside rule and yes, Charlie Buchan, a star footballer, would be screaming in his ear for change, but Chapman with a great deal of thought would do it his way and in his own good time. Patrick Barclay, in his biography of Chapman, wrote:

It is simplistic, however, to put the change down to the new offside law, and also misleading to suggest that Buchan's angriest lecture provided Chapman with a "Eureka!" moment. He was well versed in the theory of the third back ... There had been reports from elsewhere suggesting that the third back was on its way before the law change. Newcastle [were doing it], Tottenham were among the clubs who had been experimenting. Chapman was simply waiting to see what the new era taught him before responding. Now that the lesson had been harshly administered, it was time.

Chapman preferred a 3-2-2-3 formation, putting his centre-half Jack Butler back, where he could cajole the defensive ranks, organise the offside trap from slightly behind two full-backs who were now asked to look wide and look after pesky wingers.

In front of them, two half-backs, two inside forwards now withdrawn into midfield, two wingers and a centre-forward.

The new offside rule had been a quick success – the average goals per game the season after the new rule came in went up to an entertaining 3.69 – but it heralded a negative style of play. One where victory was won at any cost to entertainment. And Chapman's Arsenal garnered plenty of victories.

Other teams in England and abroad obviously followed Arsenal's example but copying for copying's sake muddied football's hitherto crystal waters. In his 1955 book, *Soccer Nemesis*, football writer Brian Glanville was under no illusions that while Arsenal were stronger for it, football's spectacle truly was not. He wrote:

> In so far as it was practised by Arsenal, the third-back game showed itself to be a strategy which, though far from spectacular, was phenomenally effective. Under the hegemony of Chapman, Arsenal's football was based on an elaborate, closely integrated defence, and forwards, who specialised in the counter attack. The example was a most unfortunate one. Spectacle and entertainment was sacrificed to results, and when other teams blindly followed Arsenal's example, though possessing none of the same resources, the consequence was an era of depressing and disjointed football which has still to end.

And how did the new system affect the new, deeper centre-half? No longer was he the swashbuckling hero of Alex Raisbeck's day, instead descriptions such as 'stopper' and 'policeman' underlined the pragmatism now required. Long passes were more *de rigueur*, centre-halves were now duelling with centre-forwards for aerial domination, but not much more. Glanville called them 'the Frankenstein's monster of modern football', going on to add that centre-half was 'the least demanding position on the field; the one player, other than the goalkeeper, on whom no constructive demands were implicitly made'.

The die was cast. Constructive demands for the pre- and post-war centre-half were limited. The third-back game was copied by other clubs, with lesser players, unable to truly do it justice, and so it became the formation of choice, meaning too many centre-halves merely went through the motions.

But it wasn't all pragmatism. Stanley Matthews, Tom Finney, Len Shackleton, Wilf Mannion: names to put a spring in the step of any eager schoolboy fan; teams like Tottenham played their attractive 'push and go' football to win the title in 1951. All were brilliant, but the centre-half was seen as the game's antichrist, hell-bent on ruin. Exceptions were Wolves' Stan Cullis before the war and Neil Franklin at Stoke after the hostilities, centre-halves wanting to give as well as take. But the norm was the rigid tower at the back. Tottenham's forward-thinking title-winning manager in 1951 was Arthur Rowe, himself a centre-half in the 1920s, who once said, 'I never scored a goal for the first team. They didn't like the centre-half to go too far over the halfway line in those days.'

'Those days' lasted for decades. The expansion of the game to a global scale was largely ignored by the English. World Cups and even the start of the European club game were ignored. Like aristocrats looking down at new money, England ignored progress, refused to believe their way was the wrong way. Soon, reality would come to town.

At the beginning of the 1952/53 season, the FA published an article in their official yearbook with the headline, 'Are We Theoretical Enough?' It was a prophetic query. 'The pupils have caught up with the teacher,' it said, highlighting the skills being shown abroad. The article went on to cite the Austrian team's progress as an attacking force and also the 'bolt' system of defence, an early use of a full-back, playing almost as a sweeper behind his full-back colleague who marks the centre-forward, with the wing-halves marking the wingers, leaving the centre-half able to roam between defensive and attacking duties, almost like a reincarnation of his Edwardian self. 'The Austrian type of centre-half,' read the article, 'is usually an astute ball player, able to join in a bout of close passing and yet ever ready to switch play by means of a long, low pass or a clever lob.' The likes of Alex Raisbeck would have been reaching for his Austrian Wiener schnitzel.

Over a year later, the Hungarians came to London, and it was clear none of the FA selectors had read their own literature. England were given a lesson by the New World order: 3–6 read the scoreboard. The schoolmasters were Ferenc Puskás and Nándor Hidegkuti, the latter famously wearing the centre-forward's number 9 shirt, but playing a deeper role and totally confusing England's back-line, finding pockets of space or creating space between the full-backs, should England's centre-half Harry Johnston choose to shadow him.

Johnston later wrote in his autobiography, 'To me, the tragedy was the utter hopelessness … being unable to do anything to alter the grim outlook.' Hungary would go on to beat England on their own turf just months later, this time 7–1. Johnston's helplessness was saved by being replaced at centre-half by Luton

Town's Syd Owen, who complained that, 'It was like playing people from outer space.' English football, the WM formation, the 'stopper' centre-half: all were relics, all had to change.

Billy Wright, the brilliant wing-half who during the 6–3 defeat to the Hungarians, according to the football writer Geoffrey Green, had 'looked like a fire engine going to the wrong fire,' was asked to convert to centre-half by the England manager, Walter Winterbottom. Wright, standing at only 5 foot 8, Winterbottom's decision was an interesting one, and spoke of football's move away from just big and physical centre-forwards and his reading of the game was vital to his new role and coping with overseas forwards with all their tactical acumen and guile.

'We couldn't live with [Hungary] and with the 1954 World Cup in Switzerland coming up, Walter had to rebuild his defence,' Wright said. 'When he asked me about moving to centre-half I wasn't entirely sure, but I had implicit faith in his judgement.'

Wright took to the position with gusto. Able to live with skilful forwards and compete with the physical. None came more physical than Wales' John Charles. Match reports suggested the duel between the two alone was worth the admission fee. England won 3–2, but Charles was at his powerful best, scoring both Welsh goals, but for all that, Wright lived with him.

'Wright clung to the task,' observed John Moynihan in *The Soccer Syndrome*, 'and one tackle when Charles had seemingly sped past him, a late slide tackle that took the ball cleanly off the Welshman's toes like a gust of wind flicking a piece of straw from a barn roof, stands out as the tackle of twenty years watching. England won 3–2 despite Charles that day, and they did so because of Wright.'

Other half-backs would make the move. Most famously, Bobby Moore, West Ham's silky young wing-half, would make his way to the centre of things. Manchester United's almost bionic Duncan Edwards was used as Matt Busby's centre-half in the 1957 FA Cup final and while tragedy meant the world never got to see just how good Edwards might have been and what position he might have consistently filled, it is an intriguing thought to think of the possible partnership he and Moore might have enjoyed at the heart of England's defence.

The very notion of playing with two centre-halves was starting to take off in England in the early 1960s. According to some, that was ridiculously late to the 'back four' party. 'You in England are playing in the style we continentals used so many years ago, with much physical strength, but no method, no technique,' was the lambasting thoughts of Helenio Herrera, the Spanish, Argentine-born coach who was no stranger to defensive tactics. 'The English are creatures of habit,' he continued. 'Tea at five.'

English eyes in 1958 had been drawn to Brazil's World Cup win with a 4-2-4 formation and in time, coaches over here began to think of refreshments other than tea. When Alf Ramsey – having in 1962 won an unlikely league championship with Ipswich using that 4-2-4 system – replaced Winterbottom as England manager, he garnered more control in matters of selection, and began to make changes to formations and how certain personnel were used.

'Alf started asking a million things about the way things had been done under Walter,' Bobby Moore would later say. 'I was playing a sort of old-fashioned right-half at the time, neither functioning properly in midfield nor in defence. I was falling between two stools and he was obviously going to sort it out.'

Not that the new man was religious in keeping Moore at centre-half. In October 1964, Belgium came to Wembley. Moore played as a half-back, and Belgium, inspired by Paul Van Himst, were unfortunate to leave with only a 2–2 draw.

Watching on was Liverpool boss Bill Shankly. Weeks later, Belgian side Anderlecht were due at Anfield. Their star man? Paul Van Himst. Something needed to be done about him. In his ranks was a young Tommy Smith, a solid and useful teenage midfielder. Prior to the game, Smith was handed the number 10 shirt, and thought he was going to be asked to play as an inside-forward. A big deal for someone so young. He was wrong. 'Shanks said we're going to shore up the defence and I would be Ron Yeats's right leg as a second centre-half,' recalled Smith. 'Great player, the big man, but no right foot. I had played up front and at inside-forward as a kid so could use the ball and I played well that night … Everyone thought that it was Alf Ramsey in 1966 who started regularly playing with two centre-backs. That's a load of shite, it was Shanks and Liverpool in 1964.'

Technically it was neither. The system had been popular abroad for many years, but with England hosting the World Cup, it was a system that would give the hosts balance, get the best out of Bobby Moore, and ultimately, help bring about glory. But who to play alongside Moore? Ramsey would decide upon a footballer approaching his thirties, and was very much in the mould of an old-school, albeit very good, 'stopper centre-half'.

In his autobiography, Jack Charlton writes that he once asked Ramsey what made him pick him, so late in his career, to play for England. 'Well, Jack,' he said, 'I have a pattern of play in my mind – and I pick the best players to fit the pattern. I don't necessarily always pick the best players, Jack.

'I've watched you play and you're quite good. You're a good tackler and you're good in the air, and I need those things. And I know you won't trust Bobby Moore.' A taken-aback Charlton argued that Moore was a wonderful player.

'Yes, Jack, but you and he are different. If Gordon Banks gives you the ball on the edge of the box, you'll give it back to him and say, "Keep the bloody thing" – but if Gordon gives the ball to Bobby, he will play through the midfield, all the way to forward position if he has to. I've watched you play and I know that as soon as Bobby goes, you'll always fill behind him. That way, if Bobby makes a mistake, you'll always cover it.'

Two centre-halves, but different. That was very much the way for a long time in British football, post-1966. And it brought some success. Celtic (managed by Jock Stein, himself an old fashioned centre-half) won the European Cup in 1967 with Billy McNeill, combative but forward-looking, and John Clark, tidy and always defensive, a player that Pelé admired saying, 'You maybe do not always notice him, but he is covering quietly for other players and always there to stop a man.' Manchester United followed suit the following year with the dominating Bill Foulkes alongside Dave Sadler, a sometime midfielder who wore the number 10 jersey and laid on Bobby Charlton's first goal in their win over Benfica.

It was a system that, in Britain at least, wouldn't change for a long time, and in many respects is still the norm today. Two centre-halves, dominating, heading, if possible one playing out from defence. Liverpool though, as they readied themselves to dominate not only the domestic game but Europe too, had newer thoughts, and like the whole English game in 1953 that looked for change following a big defeat to overseas opposition, it was a drubbing at the hands of Ajax and then Red Star Belgrade that sparked the lightbulb.

Ajax took Shankly's Liverpool to the cleaners in 1966, with a brand of new football, soon to be called 'Total', that had Shankly thinking about ways to win on the Continent. In 1973, Red Star knocked his side out of the European Cup and just months later, steps were taken to match his foes with a brand of football that concentrated more on possession and that meant starting from the back.

Shankly had Larry Lloyd, an aerially dominant and physical centre-half, with Emlyn Hughes alongside him, a sometime left-back and midfielder. The combination had worked domestically and in the UEFA Cup, but why not two totally ball-playing centre-halves? Yes, they'd have to do the dirty work too, but in Phil Thompson, a skinny midfielder who had come through the ranks, he felt he had the perfect match up with Hughes and in 1974, he put them together.

'The coming together of Emlyn and myself in that partnership was the start of Total Football,' Phil Thompson said, 'that would be made famous by the Dutch that same year. It was a clever decision by the boss and the staff. They were ahead of their time. No longer would they rely on a big, traditional centre-half like Ron Yeats or Larry Lloyd, as effective as they had been down the years. All of a sudden we were looking to build from the back. If it took 50 passes to score, we didn't care.'

It was a tactical ploy that Liverpool, under various managers, all familiar with the Shankly way, would use right up to their slump in the early 1990s. Not that it was the only way. Brian Clough's Nottingham Forest – the club who ironically took Larry Lloyd once he was deemed no longer part of the Anfield way – enjoyed great success at home and abroad using a ball-playing centre-half in Kenny Burns alongside the big man, Lloyd.

In the 1980s, 4-4-2 was king and that meant mainly two dominating centre-halves. Charles Hughes had become director of coaching at the FA and his teachings focused on direct football, stating that most goals were scored by a maximum of three passes. Budding managers like Graham Taylor took note, ambitious clubs like Wimbledon took heart. 'The only time Kenny [Dalglish] made any tactical changes to our team was Wimbledon away,' says Mark Lawrenson, half of Liverpool's centre-half partnership in the 1980s, one that bucked trends and continued to play their way out. 'We would go to Plough Lane and Kenny would say, "Right, we are playing with three centre-backs," often using Jan Molby in there. "If they are going to launch balls in on us, we need an extra body."'

The 1980s was an ugly decade for British football. Hooliganism, the mistreatment of fans, and for some a brand of football to match. It would take the World Cup in 1990 to usher in a new era, a summer where Italian opera was suddenly acceptable in a football ear, and New Order were performing football songs instead of awkward-looking players with perms and red faces. And for the centre-half of the English variety, well, they suddenly became key to the country's progress and best performance in an international championship since 1966.

'All the players had a voice, and most of the squad wanted to see a change,' says Chris Waddle of that summer. '4-4-2 was hard. Other teams were packing their midfield and we were struggling. 4-4-2 was our religion, but we needed to change and we needed to go with three at the back. I played it at Marseille and liked it. It gave everyone a lift and freed up myself and

Gazza, and David Platt. Suddenly we were the best England team since '66. We were playing great football from the back, we were passing the ball 30-odd times, and people were asking if this was really England.'

While Mark Wright, England's third centre-half in Italy, was used like a Continental sweeper, the English game did look to use three central defenders in the decade that followed. Liverpool's so-called 'Spice Boys' played a 3-5-2 with three centre-halves and wing-backs, other clubs dabbled, but success in the club game still lay with a back four, flying wingers and two forwards. Kevin Keegan's Newcastle took Alex Ferguson's Manchester United to the brink, as did Arsenal, all using a back four as their foundation.

Ferguson would try other attacking fads, going with the lone striker in the early 2000s, but his love of two centre-halves would never wane. Partnerships were key. Steve Bruce and Gary Pallister at Old Trafford were as important to his early success as Willie Miller and Alex McLeish had been at Aberdeen, and Rio Ferdinand with Nemanja Vidić would be in his later years as boss. Complementing each other, able to play the ball from the back but never overplaying. Two strong full-backs either side, support from midfield, but overall, solid, reliable, uncompromising and successful.

Successful teams since have followed suit. Chelsea's John Terry and Ricardo Carvalho, Manchester City's Vincent Kompany with Joleon Lescott and later, Aymeric Laporte, Liverpool's Virgil van Dijk winning the Champions League with Joel Matip, and then the Premier League with a dominant Joe Gomez. It's success based on intense forward play and a reliance on the few at the back to hold the fort. 'Think how we play at

Liverpool,' says Virgil van Dijk. 'We want to counter press and win the ball back as soon as possible. We have the ball up front and it is me and my partner at centre-half plus a holding midfielder making sure the organisation is right. That means every other player, especially the full-backs, can contribute to the attack and get in the box. Everyone knows their job and it is working. Even when the team is attacking, my role as a centre-half is just as important as the guys scoring all the goals.'

It seems two in a back four able to play from the back, adapting to rule changes that allow them to take the ball from the keeper in the box, stretching the play and their skills as they go, will be in vogue for a while, but watch this space. After all, they are being asked to overlap at Sheffield United, so anything is possible.

And what of the national team? England's centre-halves have long epitomised the country's tactical and technical failings but any glint of success that has come England's way has occurred when they have been used in less rigid ways. Terry Venables followed Bobby Robson's tactic of using three centre-halves in the hugely successful European Championships in 1996. On home soil, Venables switched between 4-4-2 and 3-5-2, asking Tony Adams, Gary Neville, Stuart Pearce and Gareth Southgate to switch systems, sometimes even during games.

Henry Winter, a football writer who has long observed and chronicled the national team's highs and more prevalent lows, is in no doubt that what the team does at the centre of its defence will determine any future success. 'Look at the past,' Winter says. 'Look at the Golden Generation. England boasted some of the best centre-backs around. John Terry, Rio Ferdinand, Sol Campbell, Ledley King, Jamie Carragher. All brilliant players. It's ridiculous that England didn't do better with talent like that.

'Rio Ferdinand in particular was perfect for the international game, and I know that Glenn Hoddle when he was England coach and Rio was coming through had earmarked him to play in a modern 3-5-2 system, a system that would have encouraged Rio to step out with the ball and join the midfield. Glenn lost his job though, and it was weird because under Sven [Goran-Eriksson], there was so much nervousness every time Rio showed any attacking intent. Like many English fans, it seems that too many coaches share that nervousness. That's why I like Gareth Southgate's take on the position. He encourages them to play.'

In his tenure as England manager, Southgate has tried to instil that ethos, asking his centre-halves to be more than one thing, and choosing to play a 3-5-2 in the 2016 World Cup semi-final. It seems that the England manager's final decision of who will play at the heart of his defence and how they play will determine his and the country's success. Tactically, centre-halves have become that important. When E. A. Cross took to the field, dreaming of that summer's cover drives, such a notion would have been branded mad. But that's centre-halves for you.

3

ON ME 'EAD, SON!

A Look at a Centre-Half's Most Potent Weapon ... The Head

It was Field Marshall Bernard L. Montgomery who said, 'If we lose the war in the air, we lose the war and we lose it quickly.' Not many centre-halves would disagree. Not many of a certain generation, anyway. Over the decades, our centre-halves have been tasked with countering an opponent's aerial bombardments, while marauding into enemy territory themselves with their own threat from the clouds.

The modern incarnation of the centre-half is being asked to use their head, but not necessarily by getting their foreheads dirty. At the highest level they are being asked to get a team's play going offensively, but are also repelling danger more often played in and around their feet. Concentration is key. The head is working, but not in the way it used to.

Aerial duels won are still a factor for the more vain centre-half who studies his form and stats, but should they talk to those who have played in their spots before them, they may well be told that nothing else mattered. For a centre-half to dominate his forwards, for a centre-half to dominate a game, their ability to get on top of things, literally, was paramount.

Watching these magnificent men acting like flying machines has shaped careers and history. Tony Adams stood alone on a damp and freezing sideline and marvelled at his dad playing centre-half for his local side. 'Yes, my first memory was when I was six years old, watching my dad play over on Hackney Marshes,' he says. 'The first thing I noticed was that he could head the ball very well.' It wasn't long before the boy was harbouring desires to follow in the family footsteps.

Bravery and skill. Height is a help but not a necessity, not if there is a desire to leap and to win. Fabio Cannavaro, the captain of the Italian team that won the 2006 World Cup, was not blessed with a stilt-like presence but he had a hunger to get off the ground and win that ball, meaning many taller centre-forwards were left wondering how he got his step ladder past the officials.

Paul Parker was another. Five foot 7 and predominantly a right-back, but such was his tenacity, he often played in the centre. Alex Ferguson even dropped his trusty captain, Steve Bruce, for a Champions League game against Barcelona, feeling Parker was better suited for shadowing the lively Romario. Parker was one of the great man markers. 'Paul leaps like a salmon, and tackles like a ferret,' said Bryan Robson, his first skipper at Old Trafford.

There are those of course who rely less on their salmon like springs and instead simply impose themselves on any player or situation. To look at these centre-halves is to know they are one. Tony Adams, Terry Butcher, Sami Hyypiä, Jack Charlton, players with a genetic right to be there. Brede Hangeland, once of Fulham and Crystal Palace, 6 foot 5, a Norwegian Tower of London, who in either box always looked favourite to introduce the lines on his forehead to the leather on the ball.

If Jack Charlton was brought into Alf Ramsey's England set-up to be Bobby Moore's presence off the ground, he had learnt from the very best. John Charles was at Leeds when Charlton was breaking into the team in the early 1950s. Charles, a brilliant centre-half, had been asked to take his talents to the forward line and Charlton replaced him at the back.

Charles would later be called '*il Buon Gigante*' (the Gentle Giant) by the Italian public, who fell under his charms after he signed for Juventus, but even the young Charlton managed to eke out his ire when, having listened to Charles' advice at a corner, he told him in no uncertain terms to be quiet. After the game, he found himself pinned up against a wall, with Charles, in his south Wales lilt, telling him, 'Don't ever speak to me like that again.'

Charlton heeded the big man's advice, and also took lessons in how to head the ball from a player described by the great Billy Wright as the best centre-half he had ever played against, *and* the best centre-forward. Charles' skill in both positions lay in his ability to rise above the rest. Charlton was on hand to look and to learn. 'John Charles was a team unto himself,' he would write in his autobiography. 'People often say to me, "Who was the best player you ever saw in your life?" and I answer, probably Eusébio, Di Stéfano, Cruyff, Pelé or our Bob – but the most effective player I ever saw, the one that made the most difference to the performance of the whole team, was, without question, John Charles. He could defend, he could play in midfield, he could attack. He was quick, he was a very, very strong runner, and he was the greatest header of the ball I ever saw. His power in the air was phenomenal. Normally when a player heads the ball his eyes close automatically, but John's didn't, they stayed open. If you tried to challenge John in the air, he'd always jump a fraction of a second earlier, and he seemed to hang in the air. He'd lean on you, he'd put his chest on your shoulder and lean on you, while heading the ball into the net.'

Charles was like two players in one. England's most celebrated centre-half partnership of Charlton and Moore complemented each other wonderfully, but Charles was both of them, able to read the game and able to head the ball. In Italy, his ability with both feet and cranium guided Juventus to three *scudettos*, and in 1997, their fans voted him their greatest ever foreign player.

A big man, a big presence; it was by no means novel, but to see it done so well, so powerfully, was a joy in Turin. At Leeds, his manager Frank Buckley used to stay behind after training and have him leap to head the crossbar. Not a ball in sight. Even at 6 foot 2, it was a feat, but it sprung Charles into the footballing stratosphere. His teammate in Italy, Omar Sivori, once said, 'When we were at Juve, the two most important people for most fans were the Pope and *Il Gigante*. For the 40 per cent who were communist, it was Stalin and *Il Gigante*.'

Like the Pope, Charles reached for the heavens, and thirty years later, to Italian football-goers, the sight of a British player with such aerial ability lost none of its charm. In the late 1980s, when Paul Elliott became a straight Tower of Pisa, Serie A was awash with the best of overseas talent – much of it of the attacking variety. It dawned on some that if they were to combat the likes of Mark Hateley and Ruud Gullit in the air, then they needed to buy their own anti-aircraft machines.

'They liked my all round competitiveness,' says Elliott. 'Italian centre-halves couldn't really attack the ball very well. They thought I could bring a new dimension to the team, especially at set plays. A lot of the play was set in wide areas and balls were being flung into the box. Lots of non-Italian strikers who thrived on crosses were arriving in Italy, and so my ability to meet crosses and win headers appealed to them. They were ahead of the curve to have someone who could be a marker in the Italian sense, but who had good recovery but then could command in the air.

'Italian defenders were very capable, very competent, very technical, but very few were dominant in the air. They also liked the fact that I was a big communicator. I liked to organise. Give information. A lot of Italian defenders weren't vocal. I learnt the swear words first and then after six months I was speaking the language.'

For British centre-halves over many years, heading the football was *their* language. A dialect too often scoffed at, too often taken for granted. Darren Moore, a centre-half who considered winning headers a birthright, scoffs at the snobbishness that can greet some of his kin for being able to excel at it. 'It's an art,' he says. 'An art that takes practice, bravery and skill. A keeper takes a goal-kick, he smashes it up the pitch, eighty yards, you've now got two seconds. You have to adjust your feet, get your eye line sorted, time your jump, by the time you jump you need to be about nine feet in the air to head the thing, and you are using about five inches of your head, to get it back, all with a forward challenging you robustly. Now that is a skill in itself, and people don't allude to that, they just think, oh it's just a header.

'To the naked eye it is just a header, but strip it back and goodness me. That's a skill. Neck muscles, accuracy, strength, sort out your landing, organise the back four again; you have to be so switched on, win your battles, get organised.

'I used to head the ball all game, and get distance but you can be cute and towards the end of games, if we were winning, I would enjoy looking like I was going to smash a header back but instead cushioning it back to the keeper. You can be delicate too. It can kill a game. Lovely.'

Moore describes the art of heading with a passion. In Charles Buchan's December 1951 issue of *Football Monthly*, Liverpool's Laurie Hughes did a page called 'Improve Your Game', with the headline, 'Heads You Lose – If You Don't Do it Properly'. Hughes was Liverpool's centre-half and had won the Championship in 1947, but he was quick to point out that heading the ball should not be relied upon. 'Though heading is an essential feature of the game, it should not be used only as a last resource,' he said. 'Using the head should be only a means towards getting the ball on the ground.

'So it is a good slogan – "never head the ball if it is possible to get it under control either with the chest or feet." And when the ball is headed, it should be sent downwards, either to the feet of a colleague, or at the opponent's goal. Keeping the ball in the air leads nowhere. It slows down the game and gives the opposition time to get in position.'

Such calm, practical advice seems odd from an era where the stopper centre-half had to deal with beast-like centre-forwards. It must have been hard to adhere to such advice when faced with Nat Lofthouse's intentions, and Colin Hendry, the former Blackburn and Scotland centre-half in the 1980s and 1990s, suggests simply winning the ball is all that counts: 'If unchallenged, you look to gently head it to your full-back and retain possession and build from the halfway line. If you are being challenged, up against a Mark Bright or a Niall Quinn, you just want to win the header, and if you do win it, you drop back a way as quick as you can to combat any second ball. Getting the ball back up into the air, you are then giving your strikers a chance to cause a nuisance in their half.'

It is all about winning possession and keeping it, whether that's patiently or by quickly launching an attack and by winning the aerial combats, a centre-half is ensuring the first battle has been won. 'In my day it was around the halfway line, a goal-kick,' Hendry says. 'From the floor it would be flatter, from his hands, it would be elevated and so by the time it comes down, a striker could challenge you and try to win the ball. It was something, if they were going to kick it, you could stick it right back into them, right away.

'If you win it, the opponents are unable to get up to the halfway line, so stuck halfway in their own half, and so you can really put them under pressure by winning that header. I can see why more and more people play out now, more and more today, because by doing so you are keeping possession.'

Hendry's day though saw the challenge set from pretty much every goal-kick and it was a challenge he would always relish meeting. 'It's a hard skill! The ball coming out from the skies while being challenged, it's never easy. If you are going to win the perfect defensive header, you have to tick all the boxes. Holding a line, dropping off, keeping the flight of the ball in your eye, and timing the jump.

'If the goal-kick or a place kick is flatter, generally if you time it right, the centre-back should win the header. You have a run on it, you can see the flight and generally we should be winning that. If the goal-kick was taken from the right-hand side, then I would take the right side of the forward, and vice-versa. I'll go and challenge and that just gave me a better view of the flight. It's the very first one, that's the key one. You want to win it, and you want to clean everything out. Make the forward worry, "Fuckin' hell, I'm getting this all day." You want to get it in their heads.

'Forwards are clever though. [Alan] Shearer was an expert at just standing across the centre-back, not trying to win the header necessarily, but just trying to put you off. I learnt a bit starting out as a striker. Just as the kick was taken I would know to knock the forward, you get a reaction from him and you gain an advantage. He's going to knock me so get the first one in and go from there. Put him off, and all of a sudden he's thinking. The next time he's expecting something again.'

That physical side of the aerial duel has long been part of it, but some central defenders tried to conduct themselves with a more Corinthian spirit. Ron Greenwood, Chelsea's centre-half at Chelsea in the 1950s, was known for his principles, principles that perhaps weakened his competitive edge in the air, but his outlook stuck with a young Bobby Moore, whom he later managed at West Ham.

'Ron was talking about playing centre-half for Chelsea against Matt Busby's great old Manchester United team and I asked how he coped with the terrific centre-forward of theirs, Tommy Taylor,' Moore recalled. 'Taylor was tremendous in the air but Ron said he went into the match believing he could beat him in an honest jump for the headers. The first cross came in and he got a clear sight of the ball and went up expecting to head it away. Taylor timed his jump in front of him and got the touch and United nearly scored. A few minutes later the same thing happened and Taylor scored from the header.

'So it went on through the game. Ron never changed his tactics, never tried to block Taylor's run or nudge him off his jump, not even when Taylor stuck in United's third with his head. He believed he was doing the right thing and when the last high ball of the game came into Chelsea's penalty area he went up just the same. Still trying to win his first header of the afternoon, fair and square.'

Getting a jump on the forward can be done without blocking, elbowing or nudging, although it usually isn't. Hendry recalls even getting his studs into a teammate to gain a few extra inches. 'With Tim Sherwood, my holding midfielder at Blackburn, I would have him in front of me, and if I shouted, "Stand!" he would bend his knee and I could jump off his calf. Like a ladder. I'd just get a leap off the back off his calf, his feet stuck into the ground and I could come off him to get an extra leap. Tim Flowers would do it to me in goal too.'

For plenty of centre-halves the question of how to get ahead in football isn't always an easy one to answer. Especially if you aren't used to facing centre-forwards you can file under gigantic. Frank Leboeuf arrived at Chelsea from Strasbourg in 1996, a technical player who could excel at sweeping behind such action, before showing off his passing skills. In England in the 1990s, such luxuries, while becoming sought after in an ever more international Premier League, could still raise an old-school eyebrow.

Most British centre-halves would say they preferred match day's battle to be of the physical variety, that playing against nippy, smaller strikers offered more chance of humiliation. Give them the big guys, a fair fight, anytime. For Leboeuf, playing in England for the first time, he could only think the opposite. 'When I arrived, there were so many good strikers, of all shapes and sizes,' he recalls. 'Robbie Fowler, then Michael Owen, Ian Wright, Andy Cole; all brilliant players with great movement. I liked playing them, not because I felt I was better but it was a fight I was used to. A technical fight, like I had faced in France. Now though, I was having to fight against Les Ferdinand, Niall Quinn, Duncan Ferguson. Fighting against Duncan Ferguson is a nightmare!'

Tony Cascarino, himself a nightmare inducing centre-forward with a flair for heading at goal, agrees that even the best centre-halves fear strikers who match their own aerial ability. 'Centre-forwards are not being allowed to play a certain way anymore, especially if they are big, which is rarer and rarer. Look at Andy Carroll. He isn't being used even when he plays! He has his critics, but Newcastle just don't play to his strengths. He only heads the ball from goal-kicks. What's that about?

'I know for a fact that if you asked John Terry who his hardest opponent is, he'd say Andy Carroll. Take the 2012 Cup final, when Carroll came up off the bench, and at the end of the game, despite winning, Terry looked like he'd been hit for six. I reckon Terry would not have been the centre-half he was, had he played the big centre-forwards. John didn't like playing against big men. John was great at reading the game and dealing with technical players, but had he faced the old-style forwards who liked the aerial side of things, he would have really struggled. I think it's quite sad that we no longer see a good old-fashioned ding-dong in the air between centre-halves and centre-forwards. The thing is, domestic football has become like international football now. Technical, tactical, but without that battle.'

It seems set-pieces and corners are the last battlefields left. Goalscoring can be a major part of a centre-half's game, and the use of their head in doing so is the most common method. Goalscoring centre-halves are a common breed, especially as so many of them are frustrated forwards. In England the likes of Steve Bruce at Manchester United often rattled the ball into the net, in his case often from the penalty spot, but his ability to time his run and his leap at set pieces was a big part of Alex Ferguson's early success at Manchester United.

Daniel Van Buyten, a Belgian centre-half who played for, among others, Marseille and Bayern Munich was a regular name on a game's scoresheet, grabbing twenty Bundesliga goals during his time at Munich. At 6 foot 5, Van Buyten was always going to be a threat, but there is more to it than that. Not every giant playing is a regular scorer and he obviously understood the subtleties of timing and exploiting space, always at a premium in a packed penalty box.

Colin Hendry, a striker in his early days, was always a threat in the opposing penalty box. 'It's the flight of the ball and reading that while getting a path to it that's key,' he says. 'You use teammates, it's like American football, players will block runs and you need to get through and use your teammates before timing a jump.' And woe betide the teammate taking the corner kick who doesn't deliver.

'Just clear the first fucking man! If I'm getting a taxi up for the corner kick, and I have to get a taxi back, if you don't clear the first man I'm going mad. [Graeme] Le Saux. [Jason] Wilcox, [Stuart] Ripley, all great players and great deliverers, but it was paramount they did not hit the first man. Shearer, myself, Kenny [Dalglish], [Ray] Hartford, oh, they would get stick from us all. They were generally very good though, and at Blackburn, we were dangerous because we had multiple threats.

I would look to win the header and Alan would often score with the second ball.'

Today, coaches and defenders are torn about whether to man mark at corners or go with a zonal approach, which sees players marking an area in the box, rather than a designated player. The tactic is a divisive one and Hendry for one has never been a fan. 'I don't like it, because it takes away responsibility.

'I got caught out playing against England in the European Championship play-off at Hampden in 1999. Paul Scholes scored a header from a free-kick. Scholes! The smallest man on the pitch and I got a lot of stick for it. Our manager, Craig Brown, in the dressing room went for me. "I'm not fucking picking up Paul Scholes, I'm picking up Shearer," I argued. It was Barry Ferguson who lost Scholes's run. Brown said I should have had authority to go and win it, but I wasn't having that. "Fuckin' hell, Craig, it's hard enough marking Shearer!" It's about responsibilities. Barry thought he was running into my space, but to me and the way we set up, I didn't have a space, I have a man, I have Alan Shearer. I think that's how it should be because it's black and white and you just don't let your man score.'

It's the age-old contest. Don't let your man score but maybe a centre-half's ability to use his head to do that is coming to an end. Football is changing, rules are too. With medical reports linking footballers heading the ball with dementia later in life, associations in Britain and abroad have banned the use of heading for games involving under-ten-year-olds.

Tactics too. A game between Tottenham and Liverpool in January 1985 saw the goalkeepers, Ray Clemence and Bruce Grobbelaar, kick the ball into the opponents' half 80.3 per cent of the time. In a match between the two teams in January 2020, that figure had almost halved, to 42 per cent. The big header from a big goal-kick is no longer a big weapon or a big necessity. And then there is the ball being flung into the box from the byline by a tricky winger, another nostalgic relic from a not-too-distant past.

'You just don't see it anymore,' says Harry Redknapp with a tinge of sadness. 'You don't see heading, you don't see big centre-forwards attacking the ball and attacking the centre-half. You don't see balls being thrown into the box, do you? Wingers are pulling the ball back to strikers, it's wrapped in low. There aren't duels anymore. Them great headers of the ball are few and far between.'

For those, like Redknapp, who were brought up celebrating these masters in the air, watching them gathering speed along the runway of their penalty box before ascending towards the ball and sending it on its way, the thought of that part of the game as gone forever is a melancholy one. Centre-halves, and their leaps of faith, whether they be on the local park or at the World Cup, have always got the juices flowing. They may not be around for much longer so while you can, look up to the sky and salute.

4

THE GREAT MARSHALS

What Makes Centre-Halves Great Leaders?

'I feel like I've always been a leader.' Paul Elliott, that gracious centre-half who plied his trade in England, Scotland and Italy, and was Chelsea's first skipper in the Premier League era, is discussing captaincy. 'There is something about the centre-half's position that lends itself to the responsibility. You are like the field marshal in the middle of the pitch with that peripheral view, marshalling your backline and giving information to your teammates. The real challenge for a captain is when you're having a bad day at the office, getting criticism from supporters but still having to empower and mobilise your teammates. I realised it's not what you say, it's how you say it; invest in time to understand the individual's character. While being critical is important, to highlight their upside before any negative. Understanding the composition of the human race, particularly mentally, is important.'

It is a deep take on the role of a football team's captain and how best a player – with the armband donned across their bicep – can benefit the team. Plenty of big, furrowed browed centre-halves who have been named captains might scoff at his language, might wonder about the human race's composition and how that can help win football matches, but Elliott's words are fascinating. They invite the question; why are so many who play in the position (where for so long brute strength rather than subtle thought was the prerequisite) asked to captain football teams?

Elliott has a deep air about him, and his words are indeed worldly, so let's look at the world. Of the twenty-one pairs of hands who have lifted the World Cup, eight of them have belonged to the centre-half. That's 38 per cent. A healthy majority when compared with other positions. Let's name them.

The first, in 1930, was Uruguay's José Nasazzi, followed in 1950 by his fellow countryman, Obdulio Varela. In 1958, Brazil's Hilderaldo Bellini preceded his fellow countryman Mauro Ramos, who lifted the trophy in 1962. England's Bobby Moore followed suit in 1966, Franz Beckenbauer in 1974, Daniel Passarella of Argentina in 1978 and then Fabio Cannavaro of Italy in 2006.

And what of club competition? Of the 64 captains to have won the European Cup or Champions League, 25 have been centre-halves, a similar 39 per cent. So what's it all about? Many explanations are out there. The merely positional. Where centre-halves operate gives them an unprecedented view of proceedings, a speck from which they can bark their orders, offer their support and unleash their ire.

There's also something in their characters. Arsène Wenger once mused that when buying certain players he liked to meet them first. If he was buying a centre-forward, he hoped to trace a certain air of selfishness in their personality. If meeting a centre-half, he hoped to find someone organised, someone very much keen to guide others. Ben Martin, a well-travelled centre-half who at 6 foot 7 was often the natural choice to captain his many clubs, agrees that there is something in him that enjoys the role.

'I think us centre-backs can be quite similar,' he says. 'We have characteristics that tend to make us natural captains. We're a bit different. You have to have a mindset. I think I am very stubborn in life, I like to be organised. I like to lead. I'm a control freak, basically.'

Then there's ego, sheer natural bossiness, an ability to communicate, the fact that centre-halves (used to) tend not to attract transfers and would be mainstays at their football clubs. A plethora of reasons then, dating back to the game's origins, even when our intrepid heroes at centre-half were asked to be a team's creative hub. Big, brawny and self-assured, the centre-half and his centre-half successor has always fancied himself as a leader.

José Nasazzi is regarded by many as Uruguay's finest ever footballer. On paper he played the 1930 World Cup final at right-back, but he was also a fine centre-half and that day in Montevideo that saw his country beat Argentina to win the inaugural World Cup, he was effectively the last line of defence in a 2-3-5 formation, but it was his leadership qualities that stood out.

At half-time, Uruguay were trailing 2–1 to their arch rivals. Almost 70,000 fans feared defeat on home soil but Nasazzi took the team talk, galvanising his side with words of nationalistic pride. Uruguay went on to win 4–2 and for Nasazzi, the nickname *el Gran Mariscal* (the Great Marshal) was granted and it would stick for life. He would go on to manage the national team during the war, underlining an astute understanding of the game. He remains a hero in his country today, and was followed into folklore in 1950 by Obdulio Varela, who from centre-half, captained the country to unlikely glory when Uruguay beat Brazil in the final game of the tournament to not only defy the odds but also a desperate host nation.

Brazil looked destined to win their first World Cup. Needing only a draw (the format saw a round robin selection of games), Brazilians couldn't fathom anything but glory. The newspaper *O Mundo* hailed their country as World Champions on the morning of the match. Varela bought all of his team's hotel's copies and laid them out on his bathroom floor before inviting each of his teammates to come in and urinate over their disrespectful headlines.

Later, with 200,000 people packed into Rio's Maracanã Stadium, Varela remained calm, telling his players, 'Don't look up in the air. The match is played on the ground, where we are 11 against 11.' Uruguay's eleven defied the odds and broke a nation's heart, winning 2–1. That night, with his teammates remaining in the hotel, unsure of their safety if they ventured onto the hurting streets, Varela could be found drinking beer in a bar, consoling the locals.

When you look at Nasazzi and Varela you can draw parallels with Scotland's Jock Stein, a centre-half whose ability to know football surpassed his ability to play it, but one who left a mark on a small country eager to take on the big boys.

Jock Stein was called Big Jock for reasons other than the size of his footballing brains. A coal miner, the constant scratches on his back spoke of the toils underground for a man whose frame lent itself more kindly to the discipline of central defending than that of life at the coalface. Stein played part-time football while working the Lanarkshire seams, but having given professional football a go in south Wales, a call home to Celtic – initially as a reserve – was the break this deep-rooted footballing mind needed.

Not that his arrival at the Glasgow club caused much of a ripple on the Clyde. It was 1951. Celtic Football Club were in the doldrums. No title had been won for years, and so this large centre-half walking through the gates hardly inspired thought of glorious revival. Injuries had demanded recruitment and with the hinges on the treatment room door working harder and harder, Stein was forced to make his first team debut against St Mirren at Celtic Park.

Whistles from disgruntled fans even met his name when it was announced, but Stein, as strong in mind as he was in body, played a solid game, the 7 out of 10 from the local paper speaking volumes for his no-nonsense style. 'For more than an hour this tall, well-built player staked a claim for a regular place in the first eleven,' wrote Cyril Horne of the *Glasgow Herald*. 'Before he not unexpectedly tired late in the game he displayed confidence in himself and appeared to radiate confidence amongst his defensive colleagues, and his clearing in the air and on the ground was accurate as well as lengthy.'

What the astute Horne had noticed in this solid and unremarkable footballer was an ability to lead, to lead by an ability to project his simple but deep thoughts about the game and how to win at it, to those around him. A player with a Protestant background at a Catholic club was always going to have hoops to jump through if he was to prevail in the hoops of Celtic but jump he did, and tackle and head, until in 1953, again due at first to injuries to others, he was made captain of the club he would one day manage to European Cup glory and his own immortality.

In his wonderful biography of Stein, Archie Macpherson describes Stein the player to a song in the Broadway musical *Chicago*, called 'Mr Cellophane'. The song is about a man who feels invisible, and Macpherson underlines that so little was said about Stein's playing days, despite his clear importance to the club for which he played, and the fact that he was, 'Indispensable to so many around him but paradoxically is never noticed that much.'

Macpherson continues: 'He binds, he sorts, he covers, he mends, but with little attention paid to him. It is a song that might have been written for a centre-half with a good left leg, a remarkable right knee [Stein was renowned for his clearances using his knee], a tackle that did not err on the side of caution and a soaring power in the air, all of which for the next couple of years was basic to Celtic's defence.'

As captain, Stein was the cerebral type, leading quietly by example, and, in 1954 leading Celtic to their first Scottish championship since 1938. A friend of Stein once quipped that had the big man ever fallen in the Clyde, he would have come up with a trout in his mouth, alluding to the good fortune he took with him, but there was no luck in his ability to read the game, and to teach and to lead those more than keen to follow in his steps.

One of those men was Billy McNeill. A finer player and centre-half than Stein, the young man relished his coach's words of wisdom from a young age, becoming the manager's incarnation on the field of play, able to take the many conversations he had enjoyed with Stein about the game over the years, and galvanise the ten teammates sharing his dreams of glory.

'Billy was a natural,' says his centre-half teammate, John Clark. 'It was a team full of leaders. Bobby Murdoch, Bertie Auld, Tommy Gemmell, even Jinky [Jimmy Johnstone]. They were all captains in their own right, the way they played, but in Billy, we had this presence. He was just one of the boys of course and there wasn't many club sides around who were a closer-knit group. We were like brothers, and perhaps we made it easy for Billy to captain, but when the going got tough on the pitch, Billy and his leadership qualities were what we all looked to.'

McNeill enjoyed the nickname Cesar at Celtic. For many at the club it was felt that this was a simple misspelling of the Roman emperor, but in reality McNeill and his teammates, Bertie Auld and Paddy Crerand, had been to see Frank Sinatra's *Ocean's Eleven* and named McNeill after the actor Cesar Romero, who played the movie's getaway driver – McNeill was the only one of the young footballers to have a car.

It was a nickname that, in time, proved prophetic, as such was the player's leadership qualities, fans of the famous club would forever call him Cesar. 'Big Billy just looked so imperious as he held aloft that huge trophy in the Portuguese capital with sunshine streaming down,' McNeill's teammate John Hughes said of that famous day in Lisbon when McNeill became the first Briton to lift the European Cup. 'To many of the Celtic supporters that is the most iconic image in the club's history.'

That was the thing. McNeill had the full respect of his Celtic teammates, not because they feared him, but because they admired him. They, all of them on that balmy evening in Lisbon born within Glasgow's tough city centre, admired his knowledge for the game, they admired the way he went about his career, they admired his courage to play from the back and they admired his bravery when putting bones and limbs at risk to stop opposing goals.

Sure, he could rally them verbally, and when it came to talking football few were more articulate than McNeill, but this was leadership from centre-half without fire and brimstone. Leading by example, they call it. It has been a quality enjoyed by many centre-halves given the captaincy. Billy Wright moved back to centre-half from wing-half for England and continued his steady but inspiring international career, paving the way for the one and only Bobby Moore, a player and captain whose captain's armband should have been made from silk, to match the manner in which he went about his work.

'My captain, my leader, my right-hand man,' said Sir Alf Ramsey of his centre-half. 'He was the spirit and the heartbeat of the team. A cool, calculating footballer I could trust with my life. He was the supreme professional, the best I ever worked with. Without him, England would never have won the World Cup.'

Ramsey is alluding to every manager's dream. A player not only able to read the game as if he had penned every word himself (Jock Stein once said of Moore that, 'there should be a law against him. He knows what's happening 20 minutes before everyone else'), but also a player able to carry out a coach's plans without panic or confusion. In fact, when Moore played and led, one got the impression his game needed a crisis to truly flourish. A perfect trait for any leader asked to steer men through troubled times. What did Kipling say about keeping your head while those about you are losing theirs?

When Moore died in 1993, Hugh McIlvanney paid tribute and alluded to his qualities as the coolest of heads. 'His nerve under siege was awe-inspiring. It was never simply a matter of being unfrightenable, whether confronted by physical risk or mountainous responsibility. The impression was of a nature so comfortable with challenge that it needed crisis to show its true strength. Of the supreme sports performers I have seen in action, perhaps only Muhammad Ali was a more conspicuous example of grace under pressure.'

Think of the World Cup final. England go 1–0 down to Germany. Moore sees no need for grabbing the three lions upon his chest – lions in danger of a German poaching – or to spit instructions of defiance. Instead he gets on the ball and lifts the perfect delivery for Geoff Hurst to equalise. Think of the last few moments when heads are spinning. England are 3–2 up and parts of the crowd don't even know if it is all over, but Moore demands the ball under pressure near his own penalty area, drops a shoulder and once again sends Hurst on his and the country's iconic path to glory.

'That was typical of Bobby,' says Harry Redknapp, Moore's long-term friend and teammate at West Ham. 'If I had been the manager I'd have been screaming at him to just get rid of the bloody thing, "Stick it in the bleeding stands!", but not Bobby, and as a player you couldn't help but benefit from his calm authority.

'He was special. When I got there as a fifteen-year-old, Bobby was already the main man at West Ham. He had just got the captaincy. He himself was still very young but he had to be the skipper. He had an aura about him, Bobby. When he walked into a room, it was just special. People like him don't come along very often, and his knowledge of the game made him perfect as a leader.

'He was one of the lads, no doubt about that. Everyone loved being around him but as I say there was this aura. He and Tina were this amazing-looking couple, and so his teammates looked up to this guy. He didn't need to shout at us, he didn't need to thump his chest, but he led by example. He was a quiet man. He let the manager do the shouting.

'We aspired to be like Bobby, and not only on the pitch. Everybody used to copy him. If he walked in with a new shirt, we'd all wonder where we could get one. He used to hang his key ring on his belt loop and suddenly we were all doing it. That's how it was with Mooro. He was the leader.'

A centre-half with an ability and desire to play the game tends to lead with a softer hand. Alan Hansen, like Moore, was a defender with guile who captained Kenny Dalglish's all-conquering 1980s Liverpool team, almost apologetically, with no need for histrionics. 'It was pure respect with Alan,' says Mark Lawrenson, his centre-half partner at Anfield. 'Alan certainly wasn't the shouting kind and he didn't need to bark orders. He wasn't as out there and flash as Graeme Souness (or Champagne Charlie as we called him) but he led the team with quiet authority.'

It's a gentle trait that aids success even in the pressure-raddled modern game where tensions never seem to drop below maximum. Vincent Kompany at Manchester City captained the club, not just the team, and did so with a knowing presence that Bobby Moore would have saluted. For the 2018/19 campaign, his last season at the club, Kompany spent much of its origins in the treatment room, desperate to lead on the pitch, desperate to help fend off Liverpool's now very serious challenge to his club's ascendency.

'What has annoyed me over the years is players who aren't playing, who then become sulky and negative, because football is hard enough without that energy stifling a dressing room,' he recalls. 'I tried to put my feelings and emotions aside and tried to be extra positive, trying hard to have an impact on the team that way. I don't want to put the wrong kind of pressure on my teammates because that's what negativity can do. When I didn't play, I was focused on the positive and I think that played an important role. A lot of the conversations on the bench were with Fabian Delph and Riyad Mahrez. I told Riyad, who I knew was frustrated at not playing, that if he starts complaining about his situation, it is never going to happen for him. I told him to visualise a moment, and that moment can define his season. It was hard for him, but his chance would come.'

At the climax of that very season, Leicester were giving Manchester City a stern test of their title-winning credentials and it was then that Kompany had his own moment. His stunning 25-yard hit into the very top corner effectively won the league, but it was Kompany's role as captain that night that was every bit as important as his sweet right foot.

'Into the second half, the fans were getting nervous and you sense it on the pitch,' Kompany recalls. 'You can hear it, feel it. Every chance we missed, the groans would become more audible, more desperate. Impatience is in the ground with you. You can't control the crowd, but I did wonder if my teammates would get affected by it. I started to encourage them, 'Stay calm,' was the call. I don't know if it worked and maybe I was simply shouting at myself.'

But what of the chest thumpers, the screamers, the centre-half captains with fire in their throats? Tony Adams might, maybe unfairly, come from such stock. Adams is arguably one of the great modern skippers ('Tony and John Terry are for me the best captains in the Premier League era,' says Harry Redknapp) and could make a teammate follow instructions – yes, similar to the likes of Moore and Hansen, leading by his own example, but he would also use sneers, barks and ear-splitting screams. 'I saw Tony Adams play against West Ham when he was fourteen and he was like he was when he was thirty,' says Redknapp.

'He organised, he shouted, he bossed people, he tackled. Brilliant. Are kids like that anymore? Maybe not. It's all too easy maybe. Everyone is too nice, all the players are pals. It's not right. Not at centre-half anyway! I don't know if they are coaching it out of them, are there kids like that out there anymore?'

Tony Adams actually admits to having been quite the loner as a kid. Reserved. In his shell. It was on the field of play that that shell could be broken and a domineering side of his personality unleashed. 'That's correct,' Adams says. 'I loved organising, winning and making myself look good, it was the only place I was boosting my self-esteem. I think defenders can see the whole pitch and it is then easier to get people into the right positions.'

Arsenal striker Alan Smith was one player who benefited from Adams' ability to lead and, like Redknapp, was taken by how easily he did it from a young age. 'Tony Adams was a naturally dominant person, given the armband at the age of 21,' Smith says. 'He was acting like a captain earlier than that. He played next to David O'Leary, who was the veteran and immediately told David what to do.'

No one could have coached Adams' qualities as a captain. This was a footballer so destined to lead that one can imagine his birth, and his emerging foetus giving the midwife encouragement and instruction. Many would agree that it is something a good captain is born with. Colin Hendry, former Manchester City, Blackburn and Scotland (among others) centre-half, certainly does. 'At some time or another I captained all the teams I played for, and you have to have a bit of humility,' he says.

'A captain, or a good captain, should lead by example and generally not ask a teammate to do something he can do himself.

Gary McAllister was the best player I played with and the best captain. He never asked a player to do something he could do himself. I recently did a bit for BBC radio and the journalist told me that he had spoken to a former manager of mine, who had said, "Everything was always about me." I couldn't think which of my many managers might have taken that view but I took it as an insult.'

But what if we save Hendry's feelings? Perhaps the mystery manager wasn't insulting the big defender, but instead highlighting how a centre-half, and especially one who is asked to captain a side, needs to make it all about them. A centre-half needs to dominate, a captain needs to take the pressure from their teammates; yes, why not make it all about them?

Take Terry Butcher. He was unfortunate to play the majority of his international career with Bryan Robson, England's Roy of the Rovers figure who wore the armband as if it was tattooed on. Butcher was a natural leader, though, and the image of him covered in his own blood in Sweden in 1989 is as revered in the country as any moment of footballing magic.

That night was certainly all about Butcher. A goalless draw that ensured his country's qualification for the World Cup in Italy, but the back pages the following day were all about the blood he had spilled for the cause, and his refusal to go off. Henry V and all that. Butcher was captain that night and it begs the question is someone like him asked to captain because he is the sort of man who will spill seemingly litres of blood or did he play on with the wound because he was captain?

'I was captain and so you don't quit, do you?' says Butcher. 'It was a massive game, our qualification for the World Cup depended on it, and a bit of blood wasn't going to get me off the pitch. Bobby [Robson] mentioned me going off and afterwards I said to him, if you had, I would have knocked you out. "Good job I kept you on then, Butch," he said. I loved being skipper. Even if I wasn't wearing that armband it felt natural to rally my teammates. "Caged tigers!" I used to say. It got me going anyway. I used to prowl around the dressing room shouting it. "We're caged tigers!" That pitch was our kingdom and when the whistle went, our cages were unlocked and we could show how ferocious we were. I miss it.'

Butcher misses leading and inspiring as much as he does playing the game because he's that type. Centre-halves tend to be. Peter Crouch, that most striking of strikers, recently talked about captains on his podcast, and actually called the role at a football club a 'bit of a ball-ache', citing the tedium of organising parties, chasing fines, giving out match tickets. 'If it was just the on-pitch stuff, I'd have given it a go,' he said before agreeing that in his many years at the top of the game, he felt that the centre of defence lent itself best to the job of skipper. 'I think a centre-half is the ideal position for a captain,' he says before agreeing that the game has changed, so when a skipper needs to motivate, he doesn't have to rely on sheer brutish personality. 'You don't have to be a great talker or scream and shout at people. Captains now, if they are doing their bit on the pitch, you don't need to be the Tony Adams type captain; as much as I love him and think that Tony Adams is the greatest captain that ever lived. He was a top player and he was organised and he led his back four and you always felt that he would bleed for the cause. I know that sounds a bit old-fashioned and captains have evolved now and you don't have to put your face in where boots are flying to be a leader, but it does help a little bit.'

It seems more and more from the old school to want a big centre-half willing to scream his team to glory, but Harry Redknapp has voiced his concerns about the modern game's lack of leaders. One of them who is old school in so many ways, though, is Wolverhampton centre-half and captain, Conor Coady. A sweeper very much in the old sense of the word, Coady enjoys the role of captain, even embracing all the stuff Crouch suggests as 'a ball-ache'. 'Crouchy is right, there is loads of off-field stuff to do as skipper, but I love all that,' he says.

'My wife might disagree but I like to be organised away from football and I like being vocal on the field, helping my teammates and helping my team. I'm lucky to have amazing people working with me so it's easy, they all try to do the right things to prepare for a game so my role is to just get that extra 1 per cent from them.'

It's a knowing outlook on his responsibilities, and one that would please the likes of Redknapp, perhaps persuading him that there are leaders out there today, leaders who resemble even Bobby Moore's quiet but exemplary methods. When he was coaching at Bournemouth, West Ham, Southampton, Portsmouth, Tottenham and Queens Park Rangers, Redknapp admits that his eyes would look towards the centre-half berths when choosing his main man out on the pitch. 'Yes, because you are looking for leaders,' he says. 'You're looking for characters, players who can make decisions for you on the pitch, and for some reason, yes, that player is often a centre-half.

'They don't have to be overly vocal, but you want someone who knows the game, who understands the game. I'd never have a keeper as the captain. They understand goalkeeping, they are a breed apart, crazy, yes, but they are a breed apart. Centre-backs just by the positions they take on the field, see the game, yes, their characteristics are often naturally those of good leaders, they have to communicate with players, they need to organise, and they love to moan at people. Just like us managers.

'I've had quiet ones. Sol Campbell at Portsmouth. That team was full of big personalities, potential captains. Sylvain Distin at centre-back could have done it, Lassana Diarra in midfield. But Sol had this knowing way about him and was great at it. Lifted the FA Cup! Michael Dawson at Tottenham was great for me. He was a great guy, a great person. If you wanted a player to get up the hospital to see the sick kids, Michael would be there. Ledley King too. Very quiet, but what a footballer. Very much a captain who leads with his performances, but what a player he was. The important thing is to have a captain you believe in as his manager. With belief you can let him do it how he feels is right, you have to trust him and I always trusted mine.'

Trust, leadership, eloquence, quality. There's a lot to it, and centre-halves over the years have proven more than adept at the role, despite the many different shapes and sizes that they come in. From the urinaters to the bleeders, centre-halves have got on with it, but what is never in doubt is a will to win. Even those who seem the quiet type have had it. Bobby Moore seemed the calmest of captains, but don't be fooled. Having been asked to lead out his country for the first time, in 1963 against Czechoslovakia, Moore revelled in the responsibility. 'I loved the first experience of leading England out,' he said. 'The atmosphere was magic. The crowd are fanatical in Bratislava. I decided we'd only get beat over my dead body.'

5

VIVE LA DIFFÉRENCE!

The Europeans!

The very term *Continental centre-half* can send us somewhere else, as if flicking us through the pages of a travel brochure. We are in Milan with Franco Baresi, spellbound by his timing, spellbound by his time. We are in sunny Barcelona with Gerard Piqué, a Gaudí-like tower at the heart of his and his country's defence. We are landlocked in Munich, ignoring the many efficient German centre-halves to be with Franz Beckenbauer, a footballer who redesigned defending. And we are in Amsterdam with a young Frank Rijkaard, a local ball-playing centre-half, encapsulating a whole nation's philosophy.

Let's look closer at the Dutch. After all, so many good footballing things start there. In 1995, Ruud Gullit came to Chelsea. Glenn Hoddle had played in France, played himself as Chelsea's sweeper while player-manager at Stamford Bridge, and now wanted to play Gullit there. Eyebrows were raised. This after all was the most accomplished attacking player of his generation, a powerhouse in the AC Milan and Dutch sides that lit up the late 1980s.

Gullit though had started his career in the centre of defence. Actually, to confine Gullit's football to one spot is like trying to handle water. A forward, a winger, a centre-half with marauding instincts, Gullit was every bit a total footballer, and while the sight of such attacking talent in a defensive role might have been seen as slumming it in England, his performances quickly began to turn heads and change minds.

'Ruud Gullit brought skills taken for granted in Holland and Italy to the Premiership, where the radar-controlled pass has yet to see off the longbow,' wrote David Lacey in the *Guardian*, having witnessed Gullit's debut. 'There were moments when Gullit laid off the ball at angles his new teammates didn't realise existed.'

On one occasion, early into his time at Chelsea, Gullit challenged for the ball in his own box, but his mind wasn't on a mere clearance. Instead he took the ball down on his chest, before laying it to his teammate Michael Duberry, a centre-half more longbow than radar. Gullit would later say that after laying off the cute pass, inside his own penalty area, he heard two noises. A gasp from the crowd, followed by expletives from Duberry. 'What the fuck are you doing?' came the shout, followed by a third sound, the thud of the ball being cleared into the East Stand's top tier.

More than twenty years had passed since the 1974 World Cup, but Gullit's experiences on first coming to England spoke volumes of two nations with differing ideas and ideals. While Johan Cruyff was turning the world inside out at that World Cup, those with central defending on their minds might have missed his tricks, to busy noting that the Netherlands' centre-halves were both of the footballing variety. Wim Rijsbergen and Arie Haan (Rinus Israël was their distinguished reserve) epitomised almost a decade of pure football, or Total Football as the world would call it.

In 1966, Ajax had come to Liverpool in the European Cup, winning 5–1 from the first leg. Again the talk among football's chattering classes was of the young Cruyff, but it was also a game in which the Ajax manager, Rinus Michels, gave a Barry Hulshoff his debut. Hulshoff would go on to win only twelve international caps, but as witnessed on a foggy night on Merseyside, the twenty-year-old's ability to not only shackle Roger Hunt and Ian St John but also bring the ball out into the midfield and find teammates with clever passes of differing distances was symptomatic of a changing game.

The start of the next decade saw Hulshoff and Ajax win three consecutive European Cups and Rinus Michels would take his Total Football to the national team and invigorate a planet. For Dutch central defenders a way of playing was born, a blueprint for an orange nation. In the late 1980s, Ronald Koeman and Frank Rijkaard would follow Rijsbergen and Haan's lead, first and foremost footballers, midfielders in essence able to manipulate the game and the ball, but asked to do it from centre-half. In the modern game, Virgil van Dijk is thrilling Liverpool's Kop, while Matthijs de Ligt is taking the Ajax way to Italy, where centre-halves face the sternest of scrutiny.

Van Dijk started his career in less gilded environments than the Ajax academy, and explains that life was a little different when he was learning his trade at Groningen. 'We weren't encouraged to play out of the back, whatever the circumstances,' van Dijk says. 'The big clubs like Ajax and PSV would have been coached to, no matter what, play out of the back. That was their philosophy there.

'When I was seventeen and played for the national side's under-19 squad, I was with Ajax players and PSV players, and

I started to get into that way of thinking more and more. It was then that I started to develop my ability on the ball. Before that it was different. I made big steps from there. I could mix it up because of that upbringing.'

While Cruyff and The Netherlands were creating legacies and enhancing philosophies in Germany in 1974, Pep Guardiola was only three-and-a-half years old, eyeing up the small football pitch to the side of his parents' house on the flat lands of Santpedor, in central Catalonia. Maybe his callow ears had heard the locals eulogising about Cruyff, who the year earlier had signed for Barcelona and was on his way to changing more than their line-up.

Cruyff would bring that Ajax way he had grown up with to Barcelona. As a player, he brought a want for taking risks, all over the pitch, to make those risks into acts of bravery, and acts of bravery into purity. The club to which the Dutchman arrived was not the one which (his presence is still there today) he left. '[Barcelona] were always thinking about inferiority, they had *Madriditis*,' Cruyff would later say. 'We were always thinking we were the victim but in my way of thinking there was no victim. I said: "Let's look at ourselves, let the rest do whatever they want; we know what we want."'

What they wanted, Cruyff brought them, and more. A first Spanish title in fourteen years arrived immediately but perhaps more importantly, a style, a panache, one that remains today was carved by this genius on a mission. Carles Rexach, a teammate of Cruyff's, called the changes to the club 'radical, a revolution', going on to say, 'Back then football was: "Right, out we go: come on, lads, in hard" and that was it. No one studied the opponents. It was fight, run, jump. Then it was: "No, let's play better football."

'I remember going to places like Santander, Burgos or Granada and sometimes even their own fans would have a go at their players when they fouled us. For the first time they had the chance to see a figure like Johan Cruyff in the flesh and they didn't want their centre-back to ruin the spectacle.'

Spanish football journalist Guillem Balagué agrees that perceptions in his country changed significantly, with the emergence of both Cruyff's style of play and Fernando Hierro at Real Madrid. 'When we played football in the streets as kids, the centre-back was seen as simply a defender, there to stop things,' he says. '"Just kick the ball, when you get it," we'd say to them. "We don't want you passing the ball. Let someone else do all that."'

But for Cruyff especially, centre-halves needn't spoil any spectacle. Playing with the likes of Hulshoff and Haan had taught him that, and so when he became a coach at Barcelona and once again set about rebuilding his beloved club, culminating in winning the 1992 European Cup, he did so once again by playing without fear, and that included his centre-halves.

'Johan Cruyff was not scared of anything,' Txiki Begiristain, the former Barcelona winger and part of that European Cup winning squad, recalled. 'When there are doubts, people tend to seek safety in numbers, to go with the herd. Not Cruyff. His first solution was always to be more attacking, more expansive. Three at the back and the centre-half is Ronald Koeman? Instead of full-backs, midfielders? Every time he sought a solution, he attacked more. And when he told us what he was doing, we thought: "Is he mad or what?"'

Sitting in front of that back three was Pep Guardiola, and so a dynasty was set in place, a dynasty of thought that found its way to England, where Manchester City under Guardiola have asked their centre-halves to be brave, to be what we have always thought of as Continental. At City, under Guardiola, John Stones, a British centre-half lauded for his ability on the ball, has been questioned for getting the 'British stuff' wrong: the basics, the ability to block, the hunger to stop forwards from making inroads.

Guardiola, for all his devotion to playing from the back has always sought tenacity from his centre-halves. At Barcelona, he had Gerard Piqué and Carles Puyol, followed by the conversion of Javier Mascherano from holding midfielder to central defender; all three comfortable with the ball at their feet, all able to buy into the 'tiki-taka' style of ball play demanded of them, but all unwilling to give an inch to a striker hell-bent on ruining their day.

Piqué is particularly seen as embodying the stylish football from defence that we think of when imagining the Continental. He left Manchester United, where he spent four of his younger years, due to a feeling that Sir Alex Ferguson didn't quite think his physical attributes could cut it in the English game. 'Shit,' Piqué says when looking back at his time at Old Trafford. United were playing at Bolton on a cold November afternoon in 2007. 'It was a set piece. I was supposed to be marking Nicolas Anelka. Bolton chipped the ball into the box, and I thought, I'm going to be aggressive. I jumped up to head the ball away, and I completely missed it. It was like something out of a nightmare. The ball just kept floating. It floated right over my head like a balloon. I landed and turned around in horror. Anelka controlled the ball and scored easily. We ended up losing 1–0, and it was my fault.'

After 59 minutes, Piqué was substituted and sensed his time was up, that home beckoned. 'I walked into [Ferguson's] office, and I was honest with him. I said, "Listen, I feel like I've lost your trust. Barcelona is my home. I want to go back. I hope you will let me go."' Piqué was soon winning Champions League trophies with Barcelona, and while he is one of the most aesthetic of defenders, his strength and his disgust at a forward being in any sort of space have made him the complete defender that perhaps he didn't look that day at Bolton.

Helenio Herrera, a coach who in the 1960s advocated the *catenaccio* style of defending that brought equal measures of success and supposed devilment, would have approved. He managed Barcelona for two years from 1958 and would look to Catalans for the solidity he craved. In Simon Kuper's great book, *Football Against the Enemy*, Herrera admitted to playing foreign players in attack but Catalans in defence. 'My big Catalans,' he said. 'To the Catalans I talked, "Colours of Catalonia, play for your nation," and to the foreigners I talked money.'

Not that it is only Catalonians who play their defensive role with nationalistic pride. Real Madrid's Fernando Hierro and then Sergio Ramos both played with an intense artistry akin to the Spanish centre-half. Ramos might play the pantomime villain, and his collection of red cards might match that of his medals, but his consistency, his leadership and his sheer love of a big game, games in which he tends to score as well as stop, mark him out as one of the modern greats.

Helenio Herrera would have liked him. Born in Argentina to Spanish parents, but brought up in Morocco, before moving to Paris to play football, Herrera was an internationalist who when managing enjoyed most success at Internazionale in Italy. There he made his (defensive) impact. When once asked where he might finish in an Italian popularity poll, Herrera said, 'Behind Sophia Loren, but only because she has a better figure.'

His style of play might have lacked Loren's good looks, but Italy was perfect for Herrera, especially as he began to advocate his take of *catenaccio*, a system devised by Karl Rappan, an Austrian coaching the Swiss national team. Meaning 'padlock,' *catenaccio* uses a sweeper behind two centre-halves, formerly, in the WM formation, full-backs. It allowed the opposition more of the ball, relying on swift counter-attacks, and while many saw it as a death nail in the freer-flowing form of the game, it ensured Herrera's Inter consistent success, if not plaudits.

Herrera defended his tactics in Jonathan Wilson's *Inverting the Pyramid*, saying it was only negative if badly used, citing that his methods actually encouraged attacking play from defenders. 'In my system these two [i.e. the centre-halves in front of the sweeper] were markers, but the full-backs had to attack. Facchetti, Giacinto Facchetti, could attack at Inter because of me.' When Inter were beaten by Celtic in the 1967 European Cup final, with a performance of unrelenting, attacking football ushered in a new, more attacking era, with Ajax taking Celtic and Jock Stein's methods to new heights. Celtic also played a sweeper, but unlike Herrera, John Clark in that role was the only player seemingly not interested in his opponents' half. Even Billy McNeill, his centre-half partner, would be on his way when the chance arose.

But even with *catenaccio* put in a box and placed in football's loft, Italy would idolise the defensive, would always cherish their centre-halves and a long line of links to that padlocked chain remain demigods in the country. Italy's leading sporting newspaper, *La Gazzetta dello Sport*, even gives out a 'Libero [sweeper] of the Year' award, such is the admiration for those who play from the back.

'Going there was an amazing cultural and environmental experience,' says Paul Elliott, who signed for Pisa in 1987. 'I was encouraged to play from the back as the forwards retreated and allowed you to travel, but once you got within range of the halfway line the space became very condensed and congested. There were only two foreign players per team permitted in Serie A, so world-class strikers were going out to Italy. It was very rare for defenders to go there, so I was very proud to become the first black English defender to do so.

'Italy had a rich history, producing great centre-backs who understood the dark arts of defending but were comfortable on the ball too. I think what attracted the interest was that I was also a very natural athlete, very competitive and could attack the ball both defensively and offensively so they felt with my all-round characteristics I could compete at the highest level.

'In equal measure, they respected the vocal part of my game. I was a communicator, I like to organise. This wasn't evident in the Italian game, so as my Italian evolved through having lessons and eating with my teammates in restaurants, they taught me all the basic football parlance that I needed in match-play – then the social swear words developed. In six months I was very comfortable with the language.

'My first game in 1987 was against AC Milan. My goodness, in their starting line-up were Baresi, Maldini, Ancelotti, Rijkaard, van Basten and Gullit. Napoli followed a few games later with Maradona and the great Careca. Gullit – the sheer physicality of the man – an absolute colossus but with great feet and balance – he could impact the game from any position on the field. Van Basten was the most complete striker I played against. There wasn't a weakness in his game. They were undoubtedly world-class players at their peak, underpinning Serie A as the best league in the world.'

With such talent, centre-halves had to use more than their wits to prevent space, and for as much as we glamorise the Continental centre-half, they – even the most skilful – have never shied away from more shadowy elements of central defending. To quote Sean Connery in *The Untouchables*, 'If they pull a knife, you pull a gun.'

When faced with Maradona's sharp blade at the 1982 World Cup, Italy's Claudio Gentile, tasked with man marking the twenty-one-year-old, set about his work with ruthless aplomb. Maradona's body, not just his ankles, must have resembled an ancient cave drawing, such was the tenacity with which Gentile scratched, elbowed, kicked and tripped him. Gentile in Italian means kind, and as Maradona walked off from a 2–1 defeat, kindness must have been the furthest thing from his troubled mind. He was fouled twenty-three times by Gentile alone.

Spain too have had their culprits. Today the likes of Ramos and his one-time Portuguese club teammate Pepe are considered the sheriff and deputy sheriff of Kickem, but when Andoni Goikoetxea (or 'the Butcher of Bilbao' as he was known) was around, they would have resembled choirboys.

Goikoetxea was to the tackle from behind what Cruyff was to that clever turn of his. The Basque centre-half helped Athletic Bilbao to back-to-back Spanish titles in the mid-1980s, but the crack heard around a packed Camp Nou in 1983, when he broke Maradona's ankle, almost ending his career, rang louder

▲ Nottingham Forest's **Kenny Burns** shows off an old-fashioned tackle from behind on Derby's **Andy Crawford** in 1979.

▼ Liverpool's **Mark Lawrenson** politely suggests that the referee's assistant might have made an error, during a game at Southampton in 1986.

▲ The Gentle Giant! Welshman **John Charles** plied his trade at centre-forward and centre-half, and is regarded by many as one of football's greatest headers of the ball. Here, he shows off his skill while at Leeds United.

◄ Liverpool and Scotland's **Alan Hansen** could make it look so easy, even when faced with talent such as **Peter Beardsley** and **Paul Gascoigne**.

▼ A cut above! West Bromwich Albion centre-half **John Wile** was an integral part of the club's great side in the 1970s and early 1980s; here he is spilling blood for the cause in the 1978 FA Cup semi-final defeat to Ipswich Town.

▶ Most strikers were left with the Oxford blues when they faced the duo of **Gary Briggs** (pictured) and Malcolm Shotton.

◄ 'Always centre-halves'. Sir Alex Ferguson knew that any success he hoped for was reliant on a dependable central defence. With **Steve Bruce** and **Gary Pallister**, he found just that.

▲ License to thrill! Germany's **Franz Beckenbauer** and England's **Bobby Moore** prove that centre-halves can be cool.

◀ 'A bit of blood wasn't going to get me off the pitch'. **Terry Butcher** has English hearts racing after a blood-curdling display against Sweden that saw England qualify for the 1990 World Cup.

▶ 'I say, old chap, could you possibly vacate my penalty area?' Chelsea's **John Terry** and Stoke's **Jonathan Walters** prove that the battle between centre-forward and centre-half remains an intense one in the modern game.

▲ The miracle of Istanbul in 2005 will never be forgotten, but Liverpool's European Cup win over AC Milan owes everything to the concentration and desire of **Jamie Carragher** and his defensive team-mates.

◄ England's finest. The majestic **Bobby Moore** of West Ham.

▲ 'It's an art'. West Bromwich Albion's **Darren Moore** was always a dominating presence in the air.

▲ By any means necessary! Argentina captain **Daniel Pasarella** was a South American mix of grace and grit, going to any lengths to get the better of Peru during their victorious 1978 World Cup.

◄ 'They picked on the bald guy!' France's **Frank Lebeouf** was brilliant against Brazil's **Ronaldo** in the 1998 World Cup final.

▲ The heart of a lioness! Manchester City and England's **Steph Houghton** shows off her skills at centre-half against Tottenham's **Rianna Dean** in January 2020.

▼ Adams the Redeemer. Mr. Arsenal, **Tony Adams** responds to the Highbury faithful after scoring an iconic goal in 1998.

▶ 4's **Kompany**! Belgium and Manchester City centre-half breaks the deadlock and Liverpudlian hearts with this 25-yard winner against Leicester, to help clinch the Premier League title in 2019.

▲ Both pantomime villain and serial winner, **Sergio Ramos** consoles an injured **Mohamed Salah**, having dislocated his shoulder in the early stages of the 2018 Champions League final in Kiev.

▶ A Dutch master. **Virgil van Dijk** is seen by many as the epitome of the modern centre-half.

than any success he enjoyed. He also ruptured the knee ligaments of the talented German, Bernd Schuster, and once when playing against Liverpool in the European Cup and kicking Ian Rush again and again, Sammy Lee was heard to say, 'Is there a ball on the pitch?' While he was a good footballer himself, Goikoetxea would argue that when faced with genius, anything goes.

Faced with brilliance, Italian supporters certainly have always respected their centre-halves, encouraged the way they play, however cynical it may have to be. 'Centre-backs are more celebrated in Italy,' says Paul Elliott. 'Remember, the art of defending was embedded in the Italian football culture. In my time there, I faced the very best. Look at Maradona. Maradona had magic in his feet, his left one was like a wand. It was extraordinary how he could manipulate the ball. His upper-body strength was amazing and he was just so graceful, running at speed with such control. That's the level of striker I and others faced, so of course the public respected us. More than they did in the UK.'

When Matthijs de Ligt was unveiled at Juventus, following his £67.5 million move from Ajax in 2019, the young Dutchman explained why the move was so exciting: '[Italy] it is the country that loves defending the most in the world. If you talk about Italian players, for me the most common names that come up are the defenders.'

The Dutchman has a point. List the great Italian centre-halves and you list many of the country's and the world's greatest ever players. From Cesare Maldini, AC Milan's great defender in the 1960s, to his wonderfully astute son, Paolo who while predominantly at left-back could fill in at centre-half as if born there. Franco Baresi, Gaetano Scirea, Fabio Cannavaro, small in stature but a World Cup winning captain who, according to *FourFourTwo* magazine, 'Leapt like a flea on steroids.' Then there is Giuseppe Bergomi, Alessandro Nesta and Giorgio Chiellini.

All in the Italian tradition could pass a football. The father of the Italian game, Vittorio Pozzo, manager of Italy's two consecutive pre-war World Cup wins, spent much of his younger years in England, becoming a Manchester United fan and befriending his favourite player, the centre-half, Charlie Roberts. Roberts had a knack of bringing the ball from the centre of defence and playing long, sweeping passes, and Pozzo never forgot it.

Brian Glanville, in his 1955 book, *Soccer Nemesis*, wrote, 'When [Pozzo] became *Comisario Tecnico* for the second time, in 1924, he had no hesitation in dropping Fulvio Bernardini, the idol of the Roman crowds, and a centre-half of brilliant technical ability, because he was a "carrier" and Pozzo wanted a "despatcher".'

And so, through the decades, despatch they would. Maldini (senior and junior), Baresi, Nesta, they could all pass the ball but never did so to the distracting detriment of their main duties, to tackle, to block, to prevent.

In the modern game, no one has epitomised the more robust (or should that be 'purer'?) side of defending than Giorgio Chiellini. The Juventus and Azzurri centre-half with a face like a Roman coin and an attitude to his work akin to an eager gladiator in the colosseum. Chiellini is a street-fighter. His hatred of conceding is his flick knife. He will time his tackles, execute his blocks, put his face in the way of defeat, but he also knows the darker arts, and should he use any trick he can to prevent the ball's journey ending in his goal, you will find him celebrating as if he has scored. It's a cultural norm.

Gianni Brera, Italy's most renowned football writer, once assessed that, 'The perfect match would end 0–0,' suggesting that that scoreline was a blend of defensive *and* attacking perfection, symbolising a game without error. He would have loved the 2003 Champions League final. Juventus met AC Milan at Old Trafford on a night when an Italian way of doing things came to Manchester. Like Fellini directing an episode of *Coronation Street*.

The game finished 0–0 (Milan won on penalties) but within the 120 minutes, tension, skill and central defending sent from heaven were all on show. 'Italian football is scolded for its stalemates but these teams, with ability to relish, proved how attractive an impasse can be,' wrote the *Guardian*'s Kevin McCarra from the press box.

Andriy Shevchenko, Filippo Inzaghi, Alessandro Del Piero, David Trezeguet; four strikers backed up by talent such as Rui Costa, but with each creative thrust, Juventus' Igor Tudor and Ciro Ferrara and Milan's Alessandro Nesta and Paolo Maldini left them and their talents only stifled and frustrated. It was magnificent. Maldini would lift the old trophy towards the Manchester skies that night, a former teammate of his coach, Carlo Ancelotti, and both of them former students of Arrigo Sacchi, a coach not fond of goalless draws.

Maybe it was the fact that Sacchi wasn't at all good at football, that he never played to any level and therefore didn't fear defeat, that he broke the chains of *catenaccio*. Sacchi changed the way a country thought about defending and about themselves. 'When I started, most of the attention was on the defensive phase,' he said in Jonathan Wilson's *Inverting the Pyramid*. Influenced by the great Real Madrid side of the late 1950s, and the Brazil teams that won the 1958 and 1962 World Cups, he wanted another way. 'We had a sweeper and man-markers. The attacking phase came down to intelligence and common sense of the individual and the creativity of the number ten. Italy has a defensive culture, not just in football. For centuries, everybody invaded us.'

Sacchi was more than aware of the writer Giovanni Brera's thoughts about perfection being found in goalless draws but having travelled with his father around Europe, he saw things very differently. 'It opened my mind,' he says. 'Brera used to say that Italian clubs had to focus on defending because of our diets. But I could see that in other sports we would excel and that our success proved that we were not inferior physically. And so I became convinced that the real problem was our mentality.'

Having central defenders such as Franco Baresi and Alessandro Costacurta (two mess-free defenders who simply didn't require a sweeper) would curtail any negative thoughts about a country's physicality and negativity, and with them marshalling his great Milan team's defence, Sacchi's dream of changing a country's outlook took shape.

'Even when foreign managers came to Italy, they simply adapted to the Italian way of doing things; maybe it was the language, maybe it was opportunism,' Sacchi said. 'Even Herrera. When he first arrived, he played attacking football. And then it changed. I remember a game against [Nereo] Rocco's Padova. Inter dominated. Padova crossed the halfway line three times, scored twice and hit the post. And Herrera was crucified in the media. So what did he do? He started playing with a *libero*, told

[Luis] Suárez to sit deep and hit long balls and started playing counter-attacking football. For me, *La Grande Inter* had great players, but it was the team that had just one objective: winning. But if you want to go down in history you don't just need to win, you have to entertain.'

One team that couldn't help but entertain was France's 1998 World Cup winning squad. They lacked the sheer dynamism offered to Sacchi's Milan side by Ruud Gullit and Marco van Basten but with their multiculturalism and togetherness (plus Zinedine Zidane) they had their people and the world enthralled.

At centre-half that diversity married to unity was strongly evident: Marcel Desailly and Laurent Blanc. The former, determined steel, honed in midfield, and the latter, silky artistry, honed in the south of France. In reserve was Frank Leboeuf, by now a Premier League defender at Chelsea and a player capable of being either steel or silk.

'Like so many kids, I started as a centre-forward, played a bit in midfield and it wasn't until I was twenty that I was asked to play at the back and it went well,' says Leboeuf. 'I think plenty of good centre-backs played in other positions, giving them a feel for the ball. It was certainly encouraged in France. Look at Laurent Blanc: he started as an attacking midfielder. Look at the ultimate in Germany, Franz Beckenbauer. He was a fine midfielder.' These are examples of Continental centre-halves able to use the ball as well as repel it, certainly a trait desired by the French.

When Chris Waddle went to Marseille he was struck by how comfortable the centre-halves were on the ball. 'They had an ability to judge the pass rather than just tackle,' Waddle says.

'In England they would try to stand behind the big centre-forward, go with him on the run, where in Europe, as soon as the ball was being passed, they would anticipate and get in front and take the ball away. From there they could move the team forward. It's a great skill. Unbelievable. We still don't do that very well today in England. They need to learn to get in front. I'd like to see more English youngsters with that ability. It should be coached from a young age so it becomes natural to them. Try to read the situation. Try to get in front because it's so effective. It's an art.'

Leboeuf was aware, when he arrived at Chelsea in 1996, that he was a different kind of defender to what many supporters had been used to, but he was also grateful for the more agricultural centre-halves working alongside him. 'First of all when the manager Ruud Gullit phoned me and asked me to sign I was just pleased that he knew who I was and that he appreciated me,' he laughs. 'In France I was more known as a butcher, a stopper centre-half, but when I came to England, I was seen as this good football player. Maybe it was the accent!

'There were plenty of good, ball-playing centre-backs in England when I arrived, and perhaps the likes of Gareth Southgate, who was a fantastic footballer, wasn't happy that I was being talked about as somehow different. It was unfair. I did have fun though playing with my player-manager at the back at times.

'We played in the Cup, and Ruud and I were passing the ball between ourselves, making this poor forward run, run more than he ever had. It was in the box and we were having fun with him. In the dressing room we were laughing, thinking how this guy was going crazy. Having said that, I embraced the British centre-backs I played alongside at Chelsea. Michael Duberry, Frank Sinclair or Steve Clarke were great. All were great at man marking, all of them knew what they were capable of doing and all of them knew what they were incapable of doing, and that is very important and that allowed me to be a sweeper and to be a bit more technical. You need players like that. Chris Waddle mentioned the French skill but he played with Basile Boli at Marseille. Now Basil couldn't control a ball but he was one of the best centre-backs in the world. He was biting the legs of any centre-forward he met, and they were scared of him. I loved playing with Duberry, Sinclair and Clarke. They could win the ball, I could get the ball and then I could give the ball to Dennis Wise, who would lose the ball!'

For all the Gallic flair offered by the likes of Desailly, Blanc and Leboeuf, the team that changed the world in 1998 was built far more on stoicism and togetherness than panache for panache's sake. 'It was about being compact, being a team,' says Leboeuf. 'We had Deschamps, Petit, Thuram; experienced players. We could all work together. We weren't the best players ever, the most skilful, but that wasn't what we were after. If it was, then Eric Cantona and David Ginola would have been there.

'We were able to live together, be together, everyone accepted the decision of the coach and our coach, Aimé Jacquet, created a club squad in a national team. He called me two months before the tournament. "Frank, this is easy for you," he said. "I have decided that Marcel and Laurent will play centre-half. If you are not happy then thank you and goodbye. If you accept to be the substitute, then come but never complain."'

Leboeuf did just that, and while the likes of Zidane, Deschamps and Henry shone, the side's back four (Lilian Thuram scored two in the semi-final) and the centre-halves (Blanc scored the golden goal in the round of 16) were vital to the glory that followed. 'Centre-backs will win you tournaments,' says Leboeuf. 'If you are strong, then the forwards can go and do their thing and win games. We didn't need too many chances, but with our defensive solidity, we always had a chance.'

Leboeuf's own chance would come, thanks to an opposing centre-half's actions. In the semi-final, Blanc grappled with Croatia's Slaven Bilić, and with little regard for the centre-half's union, the Croat went down to the floor as if shot, and Blanc was given the red card. 'I was on the bench and that minute was talking to a teammate, moaning about how our manager would never get us on,' recalls Leboeuf. 'The next thing I know they are screaming for me to get changed and I can see the red card.'

Blanc, a man affectionately known as 'Le President' in his country, a man whose presence against Brazil and Ronaldo in a final was surely a must if victory was to be realised. 'It was strange,' says Leboeuf. 'Of course I was sad for Laurent, but it dawned on me that I would be playing in a World Cup final. It was a bit awkward when Bilić came over and hugged me at the end, as if I paid him to go down so easily.

'Journalists asked if I was happy, and of course I was. I was going to do my best but every paper I read, or whatever radio show I listened to, or whatever TV show I watched, it was always, "We won't win without Blanc," or "We have no chance with Leboeuf." That's how important our centre-back was to the team. It was hard. I felt like a piece of shit. I said to my then wife, "If we lose this match, you and I are staying in England. We are never coming back to France." It was all on me. I was going to be blamed if France lost!'

While his own people were opposing him in the media, Leboeuf had to concentrate on his opponents on the field of play. Brazil's Ronaldo was the star of the tournament, and whatever question marks might have been raised regarding his fitness, Leboeuf had to set his mind on keeping the world's greatest goalscorer quiet. 'I'm not sure he even knew who I was!' laughs Leboeuf. 'I wasn't going to man mark Ronaldo. When there are players such as Bebeto and Rivaldo up front with him, you don't do that. What was clear was Ronaldo was going to focus his game on me though.

'In the first minute, he ran toward me. That was the instruction: get on Leboeuf. Marcel was far too experienced, world famous, and so he must have thought, "Let's go to the bald guy", I don't know. But the first challenge we had, I smashed him. That's for sure.' Let him know you are there early! Surely a tactic Leboeuf learnt in England.

As Leboeuf got on top of Ronaldo, France got on top of Brazil. 'I was keen to be tuned in from the first second, and I wanted to make sure my first touch was good and my first one against one was won. I became very relaxed and less and less concerned. The key was, when we had the ball, I wanted to know where Ronaldo was. I had to concentrate. I couldn't for one minute admire our play. Even at 2–0, I wanted to have Ronaldo's movement on my mind for the whole game. It was fun.'

The millions who frolicked along the Champs-Élysées that night and all over the country shared Leboeuf's sense of fun, but the work of their centre-halves would of course be the furthest thing from their minds. Blanc's vital goal against Paraguay, Desailly's marshalling of Christian Vieri and Roberto Baggio in the quarter-final, Leboeuf's efforts against Ronaldo in the final, these were not important. It's all about the glory. Wherever a centre-half is from, they'll know that. *C'est la vie.*

6

HE'S BEHIND YOU!

The Love/Hate Relationship between Centre-Halves and their Goalkeepers

'You should hate every goalkeeper you play with.' So says former Wimbledon centre-half Alan Reeves with unsparing certainty. Football is a game about relationships and small partnerships. Full-back and winger; midfield duos; number 10 and centre-forward; none have the enduring, familiar old husband-and-wife feel to them like that of our centre-half and his goalkeeper. Talk to those who have filled either role about the other and you will get a roll of the eye followed by a sparkle in it, as they reminisce about days gone by when like an old married couple, they got in each other's way, but when push comes to shove, they couldn't live without each other.

Reeves continues: 'Do what you like with them away from football, be best pals, but on the pitch, be it the training pitch or on a Saturday, you must hate him. Neil Sullivan at Wimbledon, great lad, good mate, but my God, we used to scream at each other, telling it how it was, that he should have come for a ball, that I should have attacked the cross. Fuck off! The thing is, though, there's a mutual respect.'

Reeves isn't shoehorning in the point about respect. It has to be there, but for some who forged careers playing in front of those strange men in green, the sands of time can erode that esteem. 'Oh, they're all mad,' laughs Kenny Burns, the former Birmingham and Nottingham Forest centre-half. 'Them and referees should be shot at birth!'

But then comes the respect. Here is a man, after all, who played and won elite silverware playing in front of Peter Shilton. 'He was some keeper,' Burns allows. 'Some keeper. Great at staying on his feet, great shot stopper ...' You sense a *but* is coming. 'But ... my God, he could moan. Typical of keepers. Peter hated crosses. He wasn't the biggest, and myself and Larry Lloyd at centre-half, we would try to protect him. Not that he ever showed us any gratitude.' There's that old married couple again.

'No, instead, he'd moan. He'd be at the referee saying he'd been fouled or injured. He'd give us bollockings all the time. If someone had a shot from forty-five yards out, Peter would be screaming at us, "Why didn't you close him down?" What, forty-five yards out? Do us a favour. Like most of them, Peter was crazy.'

Like any long marriage, there are two sides to every story, and so Richard Lee, one time custodian at Watford and Brentford, is quick to defend his goalkeeping brethren. 'They call us crazy, because we're intelligent,' he laughs. But what of this idea that a keeper and his centre-halves must dislike one another? Lee laughs again. 'I don't necessarily agree with that. The lines of communication are important. A keeper has to be audible and a good communicator, because they are the last man, and to a certain extent we can play the game for our central defenders. Yes, we have to scream but only because we are making sure everyone is doing their job.'

The likes of Kenny Burns, getting on with his tasks in front of the constantly verbal Peter Shilton, might have heard moans whereas his keeper meant only instruction, but for Shilton, what he did with his voice box was just as vital as anything he did with his hands. In a book he wrote in 1982, called *The Magnificent Obsession*, Shilton wrote, 'People see the shots I save, the crosses I take and what have you, but they don't see the confidence, determination, and discipline I can instil into a team by shouting the right things at the right time. It's got to be done. This sort of responsibility should be shared, but the man at the back – the last line of defence – should still be the dominant one. All the play is in front of him and he can see so much more than the other players.'

For so long, the English keeper, cloth-capped and stoic, was far from the screaming banshee he'd become. *Goalkeepers are Crazy* was the oft-used mantra, but while the likes of William 'Fatty' Foulke at Chelsea – all 6 foot 4 and 24 stone of him – was seen as somewhat of a circus act in the early twentieth century, he was an exception, and it was the likes of Sam Hardy at Liverpool, Aston Villa and England who represented that more quiet approach. Centre-halves and their full-backs' eardrums were saved bashings with 'safe and steady Sam'.

The 1959 *Encyclopaedia of Sport* picked out Hardy's, 'calm judgement', and that he was 'invariably in position when the shot was made'. They continued: 'He was hardly noticed on the field,' and that, 'he was as unspectacular in goal as he was quiet and modest off it.' In his book *The Outsider*, Jonathan Wilson points out that the programme for the 1913 Cup Final describes Hardy as, 'confident and reliable ... Exceptionally cool in action, and clever in anticipation, and with sound judgement.'

Perhaps it was the fashion for a third back, a centre-half, that changed keepers from the Edwardian reliable, sound, unspectacular types, and with a new defender there to both protect and infuriate, goalkeepers slowly started to come out from their shells. Frank Swift, the pre- and post-war Manchester City keeper, was widely seen as a great, but that same 1959 *Encyclopaedia of Sport* had reservations about one personality trait. 'Swift might have been the greatest of all time, but for a tendency for showmanship,' it wrote.

Showmanship wouldn't do. Not in prudish, 1950s England, with its Tupperware-grey outlook on most things, let alone footballing goalkeepers, but times, they were a changing and a new crop of young keepers was emerging. Greased hair, a wanderlust attitude when it came to old habits of staying on their line and the knowledge that their Continental cousins were reinventing their position and how they played with their defenders; these were the new wild ones. And our centre-halves had better get used to it.

Actually these new-fangled keepers with their wild ideas could come in handy. Like so much in the English game and it's way of thinking, attitudes began to drastically change after Hungary's dismantling of England and its beliefs in 1953. While Puskás, Hidegkuti and Kocsis rampaged around England's defence like ants at a sugary picnic, Hungary's keeper Gyula Grosics was doing his own bit to rewrite the game's copybook. 'Unorthodox but effective' was how the commentator Kenneth Wolstenholme worded it with English pragmatism when Grosics came marching out to the edge of his penalty area to clear the danger.

Brian Glanville later noted, '[Grosics] never hesitated to dash out of his penalty area, thus frequently becoming the extra full-back. Since his timing is generally shrewd, the effect was to decrease to some extent the burden placed on the rest of the defence by the advanced position of the inside-forwards'. Decreasing the burden? That sounds handy, and Grosics himself, years later, would write about his renown for, 'running out of goal to meet an oncoming attacker or, in other words playing as a fourth back'.

In Hungary the third back (the 'centre-half' in England) was just a third 'full-back' and to Grosics the relationship was vital. In *The Gillette Book of Cricket and Football*, published in 1963, he wrote: 'Harmony between the full-backs and the goalkeeper is of the greatest importance. A basic condition of efficient team work between the four players is the thorough knowledge of each other's style of play. For this purpose, there must be frequent talks between the goalkeepers and the full-backs at which the reasons for a successful or unsuccessful sortie from the goal can be analysed and suitable preparations made for adapting themselves to the style of play of the next opponent's forward line.'

Young bucks taking note included Peter Bonetti at Chelsea, Tommy Lawrence at Liverpool and Pat Jennings, a former Gaelic footballer, signed by Tottenham. Lawrence especially embodied the buzzword doing the rounds of 'sweeper keeper'. 'He comes so far off his line he plays like a defender,' commented the then Manchester City manager Joe Mercer. It was a tradition that remained at Liverpool through their most successful period at home and abroad, with Ray Clemence and then the more than trigger-happy Bruce Grobbelaar following Lawrence's lead and becoming an auxiliary member of the back four.

'Bruce was a one-off,' says Steve Nicol, who occasionally played at centre-half in front of him. 'A total nutter who took some getting used to, but we knew he could play. It was pretty straightforward. If there was a certain ball played in, Bruce was coming for it. There were errors, especially early on. We learnt the hard way, but Bob [Paisley] persevered with him and in time, us defenders knew that if a ball came into a certain area, Bruce was coming to get it.'

Many in the game took the new back pass rule (which prohibited keepers picking up passes back to the keeper) as a factor in Liverpool's demise in that decade. Whether that is true or not is up for debate, but what is clear is that the relationship between keeper and centre-half became more nuanced. Keepers would have to play a bit too, and the better they are at it, the more accomplished the team will be.

The Dutchman Edwin van der Sar at Manchester United took his teachings at Ajax and prospered. 'When the opposition put pressure on the defenders, they played the ball back to you, and you looked for a teammate who was available to play it to,' he later said. 'If there was no option and someone was pressurising, it was played forward, but you were always looking to keep possession.'

It was a rule that made all keepers potential sweeper-keepers, and van der Sar was one of the very best around. 'If your defenders aren't quick, it's not a good thing to defend too high up the pitch, because if the opposition have a fast striker, every ball's over the top and they're gone,' he said. 'You have to look at the quality of your back four and keeper, and take it from there. If your back four moves ten yards forward, you have to move ten yards forward with them, make sure you get the little through balls and kick the ball away or keep possession.

'It's important to be able to use your feet. If your teammates know you can play, they feel comfortable with you behind them. They know if they're in trouble they can play the ball back and it's not going to be a wild kick up front or out but that you can keep possession for them and play the ball forward ... I remember when the back pass rule was announced and the next day we started practising not using our hands any more, with defenders helping. When the ball was played back they were going wide, and we got three or four opportunities to pass to them, to the left, to the middle or to the right, or the long one ... nowadays keepers have to be able to do that.'

So, today more communication is necessary. The connection between centre-half and the custodian behind him is even more vital, and with that there is even more reason to fall out? Pat Jennings, the first player to play a thousand professional games, mainly for Tottenham and Arsenal, doesn't agree with Alan Reeves' quip about the two positions' need of a level of hatred, instead talking warmly about his link with those placed there to protect his goal.

'My relationship with my centre-halves was the most important I had in any team,' he says. 'I would immediately try to get to know the centre-half's game. Was he quick? Was he not, and therefore would he like to drop deeper? Was he a good reader of the game? Was he dominant in the air? By knowing his game, I could add to it and that would help mine.'

Still coaching young keepers, what does Jennings make of what a modern number one has to be able to do in regard to actually knocking the ball about with his defenders? 'I was good with my feet but only in terms of making saves,' he says. 'Keepers today have to be able to play, but it still amazes me when I see them knocking the ball about with central defenders and full-backs in their area. If I am playing, and I see the ball being played about at the other end of the pitch, I'm more than happy as the ball is as far away from me and my area as possible.'

Jennings makes an interesting point. The goal-kick. A punt upfield or something more tactical? It used to be a way of getting the ball into the opponents' half, teams would then scrap for the second ball and attacks were formed one way or another. Writing those words with the backdrop of today's need for attacks starting from the back seems a tad archaic but for many – including much of Jennings' generation – football is a territorial game, and for many of the pretty patterns made by the top, top clubs and their coaches (with all due respect to lesser teams and their players), it still very much is.

Nicky Weaver, once the goalkeeper at Manchester City, today coaches at Sheffield Wednesday and is quick to underline the point that not every keeper can be so precise in starting his own team's attacking thoughts. 'The Championship, where I work, is a different thing to the Premier League and the Champions League,' he says. 'Yes, there is a difference in quality, but the pace is even more frantic, forwards set traps and get at keepers and centre-backs and unless you are spot on with your passing from the back you will be punished. It's great to see the top teams, City, Liverpool, even Leicester, doing it and beating a press using the keeper and his centre-backs, but it's not the be-all and end-all.'

The idea that a keeper was there to do anything other than catch the ball and kick it long was still relatively new in the post-war game. Foreign keepers who looked to be more involved were deemed flashy and extravagant by conservative observers in

England, as if commenting on French cuisine rather than tripe. It was one of Weaver's esteemed predecessors at City, Frank Swift, who changed some minds. Yes, he was also deemed flash but his eagerness with ball in hand to do more than merely punt it into the sky, and instead build attacks, was noted by those looking on.

In the 1950 book *Soccer from the Press Box*, the writers Archie Ledbrooke and Edgar Turner talk of the change in Swift after the war and how useful his new tactic was to his team and his country: 'Swift emerged as the complete team man, able to use the ball. It was, like all good ideas, simple in its conception. Having obtained the ball, he had to give it to a teammate, and for this purpose Frank Swift employed several devices. The most spectacular was the long drop kick, which he mastered to such an extent that in one match he was able to land the ball at Matthews' feet half a dozen times, the ball flying low and truly like a well-hit golf-drive.'

Today, keepers use various methods of getting an attack started. Some far more subtle than a drilled kick or a long throw. Keepers, in order to get the ball to a centre-half, will drop a shoulder, sell an onrushing striker a dummy, play a one-two. Fans gasp before applauding, wishing their players wouldn't be so gung-ho while also nervously cheering the striker's embarrassment at being 'done' by a mere goalie.

Nicky Weaver though is quick to point out that there is still a place for getting the ball out, into the opposition's last third as quickly as possible. 'When I started out,' he says, 'us keepers would chip the ball up to the halfway line. Look at the likes of Kasper Schmeichel today: he drills it to a few yards of the eighteen-yard line, and let's not get all snobbish about it, Manchester City are brilliant to watch, and the way their keeper,

Ederson, can play with his defenders with the ball at his feet is incredible, but watch him, when he gets the ball his immediate thought is to go forward with a long ball. Not a long aimless punt, but his skill is his long-range passing and he will look for Agüero or Sterling with a seventy-yard pass.'

Like thumbs growing on a primate, the evolutionary desire from keepers to join in brought the need for a deeper relationship between him and his central defenders. Neither need be merely in the demolition game. Construction beckoned too. With these new roles came a deeper relationship between them, and so is born the marriage analogy for to make this work, words such as communication and trust now had to be used.

'The longer you play with a centre-back, you build up an understanding,' says Nicky Weaver. 'Keepers can have different shouts and different calls, and talk in a slightly different way and we get to know a defender's traits. Do they like to attack it, do they like to drop off? You build up a trust.

'My last season at City I was behind Dunny [Richard Dunne] on the right, Sylvain Distin on the left and it worked so well. Both good in the air, both had a turn of pace, but what was great was they were right- and left-footed, so I could play it to Sylvain and he would take it with his left. If you don't have that balance, sometimes they take the ball and come inside and you might have a problem. There's all sorts of things but the more you play together, the better understanding you all get and most importantly, there is that trust. I think a keeper and his two centre-backs must have that trust.'

Richard Lee agrees and – sorry, but the marriage and relationship analogy won't go away – he also points out that for things to thrive between the positions, there must be an ability and a willingness to listen. 'So many goals that go in are because of a breakdown in communication,' he says. 'That might not go noticed by fans and by pundits but it will be noticed by the defending goalkeeper and tempers might be lost.

'You don't have to necessarily have some unbreakable bond, players move from club to club and have to hit the ground running, but it was always great to play behind a centre-back who listened, a centre-back who heard your instructions, the info you were giving them and acted on it. Ultimately and ideally, they trusted what you were telling them.'

Centre-halves and the bashing that their ears will take will depend on the character of the goalkeeper behind them. Steve Bruce and Gary Pallister might have been the pillars on which Alex Ferguson's success was built, but plying their trade in firm earshot of Peter Schmeichel's vocal cords must have sometimes had them wondering if that plethora of silverware was worth the pain.

'It's true, Schmeichel when he was playing seemed like he was having a constant argument,' says Lee, before going on to defend his right to do so. 'More often than not, the best keepers have quite an analytical mindset, seeing things as they develop and predicting things before they develop. They see things that maybe the defenders aren't necessarily seeing. A keeper needs the ability to offer those short, sharp and concise nuggets of information and a good knowledge of the game. Being very assertive is key too. Not aggressive, although some are, but assertive.'

If Bruce and Pallister had to get used to Danish tongue-lashings, Tony Adams and his partners at Arsenal had life a little easier, though not to the detriment of their success. 'I played with both David Seaman and Peter Schmeichel and they were polar opposites,' says Nicky Weaver. 'David was quiet and calm, just chewing on his chewing gum. Peter was never calm or quiet. You didn't want to get on the wrong side of him on a match day. Both were brilliant but both had different approaches to the way they talked to their centre-halves. I was more the Seaman type.'

And it works both ways. A keeper who is the quiet sort might have to put up with a more boisterous kind of character in front of him. Nicky Weaver knows the type: 'I played with a guy called Andy Morrison at Manchester City and he would get himself so wound up before a game. He'd be doing all sorts to gee himself up and he'd look at me and say, "Come on, get yourself going, lad," but I'd be all, "No, I'm alright thanks, Andy." I am happy to chill out in the corner while he was beating his chest.'

If we are to see our centre-half and their relationship with a keeper as a marriage, we have to say it is of the arranged variety. Put together by managers rather than parents, but given the opportunity to find their one true love, what would each choose in their perfect partner?

Joe Worrall, the young Nottingham Forest and sometime England under-21 captain, wants a keeper who talks but can also use his feet. 'Yes, I want noise and instructions,' says Worrall. 'But I want to be able to pass the ball back to the keeper and I expect him to get it into the opposition's half. I hate it when a keeper can't kick far because all you want as a defender is the pressure to come off for a bit. Yes, I want the keeper to be commanding, but that is his job. I want to trust the guy. You don't hear anyone saying a right winger is really trustworthy. No, they don't need to be. I want my keeper to be though.

'He doesn't have to be massive. It's about presence. You want the attackers to know that if the ball comes in the box, my keeper is taking everyone out to get the ball. Acrobatic saves are nice but they are meant to do them. That's their job. It's about filling me with confidence. If I get beaten, I still want a get-out-of-jail-free card.

'If I am playing in front of a seventeen-year-old academy guy, my game will change that day because I'll be worrying about him and trying to look after him, coaxing him, worrying that he's OK. What I need is consistency. We all want to keep the ball out of the net, and we have to trust each other and know each other.'

For Richard Lee, looks mean a lot. 'Physicality is vital,' he says of his ideal centre-half. 'You need to be tall, physical, strong.' Nicky Weaver takes it on another level: 'When I think of centre-backs, I think of a big guy with a broken nose and a few black eyes over the years. But that's a bit old school because it's not quite like that anymore. No one gets their elbows out these days. I wouldn't want to meet a new centre-back who was pretty. Wingers or a centre-midfielders maybe, but not a central defender. In my day we expected a few scars, a split lip and a scarred brow. No pretty boys, please!'

But enough of such superficial traits. What do they want from the player himself? 'I liked a centre-back who was quick on the turn,' says Richard Lee. 'Powerful and dynamic too. Willing to listen but at the same time assertive themselves in how they play. Also, a calmness is key. Unlike other positions, they need to be analytical as well and be calm with it, whatever is being thrown at you. Even if they are not captains – and so many make good captains – they need to be leaders.'

When picturing his perfect centre-half, Nicky Weaver points to traits in play as well as shared beliefs. 'Being good in the air is vital,' he says. 'Pace is nice but I wouldn't say it is a necessity.

A slower centre-back might read the game better and make his challenges by being in the right place and not solely relying on pure pace. Those guys often make the better player. You also need to share that desire to keep a clean sheet. That's like a goal for a keeper so you want central defenders that share that desire not to concede. In today's stat-based game, keepers probably feel that even more keenly than my generation.'

And what of the real dislikes between the positions? The annoying idiosyncrasies that can muddy even the calmest of marital waters?

'I didn't like it when they give you a back pass with no thought for your next move,' says Weaver. 'Play it to you willy-nilly, to your weaker foot, or with some spin, and then without giving you an angle for a return pass. That annoys me. The ball is spinning and bouncing and making a keeper think about his first touch. Coaching, I see it now. Also, block the forwards run with a little arm. Give me an extra second. They get lazy sometimes and that's annoying.'

Richard Lee is quick to find faults too. 'Those that didn't listen were the biggest bugbear. You have problems however good you both are, but no chat between you and you have big problems. I didn't like the central defenders who refused to take responsibility. There is nothing worse, and I had a couple of these who, when a goal was conceded, would come and pat you on the back as if to show the crowd that it was your fault. Even though he was at fault too. I hated that! Look at me, Mr Nice Guy.

'Also the con men. Without naming names, certain centre-backs can have a great profile and everyone may think they are this commanding figure but to their teammates, they will hate playing with them because they, and the untrained eye, might not notice this, but they make it all about them, even though they don't have a clue about real defending. They are the guys who get caught on the wrong side of a striker, or caught out of position, but because they sometimes salvage it with a last-gasp block, the crowd cheer them and their reputation is enhanced. A last-gasp block is often a symptom of bad defending.'

So there must be a bond, there must be communication and there must be trust. There are bugbears, there are real dislikes, even hatred and breakups are sometimes inevitable. The relationship between our central defenders and the goalkeeper is a complex, multilayered one that demands a connection.

Alan Reeves, the Wimbledon defender who suggested that, on the pitch at least, there must be a degree of hatred, finishes the chapter with a story. 'Wimbledon were playing Aston Villa at Selhurst Park,' he recalls. 'I went to clear a cross, but it bobbled, hit my toe and went in the top corner. Twenty-eight thousand people watching and I have done that. Sympathy? My head is in my hands, Sully [Wimbledon keeper Neil Sullivan] has his gloves over his face – not because he is sharing in my pain, distraught for his teammate – no, he is laughing his head off. What a twat.'

7

THE DARK ARTS

How Centre-Halves Bend the Rules

It was a rite of passage. A footballing bar mitzvah, if you like. For a certain generation of player, the day your hitherto unmarked face met an opponent's sly elbow, or the back of your head was introduced to an adversary's furrowed brow, it meant you had made it and were now very much part of football's dark and often violent world.

Coaches and their manuals might teach football's skill set, ways of harnessing a player's talent and improving the way they play the game, but it was through sheer (and literal) bloody experience that a footballer learnt that much of their time on the football field was going to be spent both giving and taking a certain amount of what can be affectionately known as 'the rough stuff'.

Football's dark arts have long been part of our centre-half's arsenal. Traditionally not the most skilful player on the pitch, a centre-half is in the business of preventing skill. Something has to give and for generations, that prevention came from methods outside of the game's rule book.

'I remember my first time,' says Chris Waddle, a player who while seeking space, could make a centre-half look particularly foolish, and frankly that wouldn't do. 'It was in training at Newcastle. I was a young lad, showing off, trying to impress the manager. We had a good centre-half, very typical of the late 1970s. Stuart Boam was his name. Hard. I'm doing all my step-overs and tricks, and crack, I'm on the floor. Stuart is standing over me. "Listen, kid, I get a good bonus if I play Saturday, and you doing all that and taking the piss out of me, making me look silly, might stop that happening. Cut it out." My lesson was learnt.'

Mark Bright, a player who came up the ranks of lower-league football in the late 1970s before scoring top flight goals at Crystal Palace and Sheffield Wednesday, was used to hard men marking him, but didn't experience the sneakier side of things until he was marked by Slaven Bilić in the 1990s. 'Everyone learns them from someone,' Bright says, 'and Slaven Bilić was the first player who wrapped his arms around me on a corner. He let go as soon as the ball was cleared. I was shocked. He looked and said, "It's the Continental way." I said, "I'll show you something English in a minute."'

For today's footballing public, their eyes aided by cameras at every conceivable angle and fuelled by their demand for fair play (perhaps when it suits their team), the idea of a player punched, pinched, kicked, trod on, spat at or grabbed by the genitals must seem archaic, a leftover from the days when the pitches weren't green, and the antics that went on them were as dirty as the kits the players wore from the field.

'My first league game I was marking Joe Jordan at Bristol City,' recalls ex-Wimbledon centre-half Alan Reeves. 'First minute, no attempt to get the ball, he just elbowed me in the nose. Everyone's too nice these days. All that handshaking before the game. Someone like Mick Hartford would have had a nail in his hand!'

Even Hartford himself, a centre-forward able to terrorise with both his ability and his aggression, but adamant that he was brave, not hard, had to learn the hard way. 'The biggest education was at Lincoln,' he recalls. 'I was playing in the Lincolnshire Senior Cup and faced Scunthorpe. I made an early run across the centre-half, and I woke up about five minutes later.

'The guy had smashed my nose in with his elbow. The physio said, "You're coming off," which was something back then too, and I said, "No, I am OK," but he wasn't having it: "Your nose is in a bad way." I got into the dressing room and looked in the mirror and my nose was all over my face. From that day on, I thought, I am going to look after myself.'

Hartford isn't alone. Alan Smith, the former Leicester, Arsenal and England centre-forward, is another who recalls the nastier side of 1980s football. 'There were a lot of tough centre-halves,' he says, with slight understatement. 'Some were fair. Mick McCarthy, for example. Very hard, but not sneaky. Tough, but honest. Graham Roberts at Tottenham too, but his partner Paul Miller was sneaky. If the ball was up the other end, he wasn't averse to elbowing you in the throat as you stood side by side watching the play going on up the other end. Gordon McQueen too.

'Manchester United played at Filbert Street once and off the ball, McQueen elbowed Peter Eastoe in his face and shattered his jawbone. Peter was sucking through a straw for ten weeks after that. These are the kind of things that went on without cameras around.'

When it came to protecting yourself or your goal, *by any means necessary* was the norm. Footballers sporting their toothless grins might be a bygone image, but don't be fooled that the dark arts are no longer used in today's high-pitched version of itself. The sight of a Billy Bremner going to toe to toe with Dave Mackay might be of another age, but the use of methods apparently not taught in football's training pitches still exists, and some might argue it is as unscrupulous as ever. The sly punch to the kidney of yesteryear, or diving in the penalty area? Fine lines.

'I'm 100 per cent jealous of my central defensive predecessors who were able to tackle from behind and leave a bit on a striker,' laughs Joe Worrall, Nottingham Forest's young centre-half and former England under-21 captain. 'I do understand the rules are there to protect me too, and no one wants to see people get hurt, but I have looked at football in the past and thought, that looks fun! I've only played 100-odd games but I do think about how the game is changing.

'You can't touch players anymore. I'm not just saying that as a defender. I feel for big strikers too. The game is suffering a bit too. We played Cardiff recently and in the second half, the ball was in play twenty-eight minutes. That's ridiculous. That shows how much players are going down and looking to win free-kicks because the rules specify that contact equals a free-kick.

'You can't even head through the back of someone, you can't raise your arms, and that's changed from even my youth team days. That's only five or six years ago, but you could put yourself about a bit. I'm not somebody who goes onto a pitch with a mindset to hurt someone. I never have, I do like the physical battle but you can't get away with things like you used to. Football today is in HD!

'I'm a massive Nottingham Forest fan and have watched videos of Kenny Burns and the 1980 European Cup final stands out. Forest played Hamburg and what struck me about it was Burns absolutely pummels Kevin Keegan. For the first ten minutes, Kenny smashes him. He doesn't care about the ball, it's just laying his mark on Keegan, kicking him, kneeing him. He must have been told. Sadly that's not in the game anymore.'

Kenny Burns himself brims with pride that today's generation – a generation he readily admits he thinks are 'too fucking nice' – appreciate his actions. 'He's right,' Burns says. 'I was told to get into Kevin from the off that night and that's exactly what I did. There was a 50-50 and whack, I hit him hard, left a bit on him, and while Kevin wasn't the type to moan, as the game went on, he started dropping deeper and deeper away from me, until towards the end, he was getting the ball off his keeper. That's fine by me. Their best player deep in their own half? That's a battle I've won then.'

'Battles', 'being in the trenches', 'the scars of war'; militaristic terms readily used in British football, peaking in the 1960s, 1970s and 1980s, when the centre-half used a range of 'weapons' to win his personal duel. There were the big guns; the hefty tackles from behind, and the knee-high kicks, but there was also war by stealth, the studs scraped along an Achilles, the punch off the ball, spitting. By the time Burns hatched his plan to see off the threat of Kevin Keegan, the dark arts – both the obvious and the sly – were very much the norm.

Fourteen years earlier, England had become world champions, led by Bobby Moore, his hair and image as golden as the Jules Rimet trophy that he held aloft. Moore's ability on the ball was the talk of the planet. Like a new Beatles album or an E-Type Jaguar, England's number 6 was an English institution, a symbol of cool, admired at home and from afar. But his skill and his supposed dedication to fair play weren't setting trends. No, there were forwards to be stopped and games to be won. The advent of a wingless formation concentrated the battle infield. Two centre-halves, two strikers. Ding-ding, seconds out, round 1.

Moore's centre-half partner in 1966 was Jack Charlton, a late bloomer in terms of international football, and very much the yang to Moore's yin. Taken under the wing of John Charles at Leeds, Charlton had all of the big Welshman's heart, but if Charles was known as the 'Gentle Giant', Charlton had no time for the gentle bit. An old-fashioned stopper, a fantastic organiser of a back four, and a tackler of keen ferocity, Charlton epitomised the position, but also the retribution that was a hallmark of the time.

'I've got a little black book,' Charlton said while playing, 'in which I keep the names of all the players I've got to get before I pack up playing. If I get half a chance they will finish up over the touchline.' Vendettas and settled scores were as common on the pitches of England at the time as the hills of Sicily, and even family ties couldn't prevent the bloodshed.

In the 1965 FA Cup semi-final between Leeds and Manchester United, Jack Charlton faced his younger brother Bobby, and if blood is thicker than water, then the thought of Wembley's twin towers is thicker than blood. With the ball bouncing about, Bobby had to contemplate a 50-50 challenge with Charlton's defensive partner, Norman 'bites your legs' Hunter. 'My first instinct was to settle for being second best,' recalled Bobby Charlton. 'Realising how shameful that would be with "Our Kid", my brother Jack, playing for Leeds and my parents watching, I was tempted to be brave. Then I heard a familiar Geordie voice. "Clatter the little bastard," yelled

Our Kid. I pulled out, deciding in an instant not to offer Norman the opportunity.'

Charlton replaced the great John Charles as Leeds' centre-half, and brought a different approach to how best to deal with his centre-forward foe. Charles was dubbed the 'Gentle Giant' while in Italy, due to his total dependence on fair play – a little easier when you are 6 foot 2 and seemingly carved from the rich seams of coal that lay under his hometown near Swansea.

Charlton though saw close hand that Charles, while fair, was very, very hard. 'He'd never go through somebody or kick them from behind, as centre-backs often did in our day,' Charlton noted. 'But John used to run with his arms stretched out, and he was so big and strong, you just couldn't get close to him without being whacked. I remember one guy getting too close to him and being knocked clean over by these massive, powerful arms.

'They may have called him the Gentle Giant – but when it came to the tricks of the trade, John was right up there with the best of them.'

In the 1960s, opportunities for retribution were always on offer to a centre-half with revenge on his mind. Tommy Smith, 'the Anfield iron', never shy when it came to encounters on the field of play, underlined the mindset at the time when he recalled an encounter with Calvin Palmer of Stoke. 'He once butted me at Anfield in front of the Kop,' he said. 'He cut me above the eye – he was only a little fella, so he had to jump to do it. Mind you, I did get him back when we were down at Stoke a couple of months later. It wasn't a case of an eye for an eye but it was definitely a case of a tooth for a tooth, I can assure you.'

Don't be fooled. It wasn't only the likes of Smith, Hunter and Charlton at centre-half dishing it out. Even the most blue-eyed hero had to look after himself. 'Somebody would come and kick a lump out of Bobby,' Geoff Hurst said of his teammate and captain, Bobby Moore. 'He'd play on as if he hadn't noticed. But ten minutes later ... *Whoof!* ... He had a great "golden boy" image, Moore, but he was hard.'

Images of Tottenham's Dave Mackay grabbing Billy Bremner by his footballing lapels in 1966, and the constant sight of George Best's ankles, polka dotted with stud marks like olives in a martini, it was as if foul play had become fashionable. Expected. Accepted. For some, it didn't sit right. In 1969, Manchester United manager Matt Busby wrote an article in the *Observer*, highlighting his concerns:

The way things are going alarms me deeply. Hard men are nothing new in football. What is new and frightening about the present situation is that you have entire sides that have physical hardness for their main asset. They use strength and fitness to neutralise skill and the unfortunate truth is that all too often it can be done. Of course, there are really great players who cannot be subdued all the time, but their talents are seen only in flashes and they have to live dangerously. George Best survives only because his incredible balance allows him to ride some of the impact of some of the tackles he has to take. Because of their heart and skill, he and other outstanding players in the league can go on giving the crowds entertainment. And it's true there are still a few teams who believe the game is about talent and technique and imagination, but for any one you'll find ten who rely on runners and hard men.

Not that all managers shared Busby's puritan approach. Even Busby himself would seemingly contradict his concerns when, in the August of 1969, Manchester United, by now managed by Wilf McGuinness, bought Ian Ure from Arsenal. A signing sanctioned and organised by Busby. The reasons for signing the big Scot were seemingly combative. The season before, Ure had stood up to Denis Law, a striker who made up for what he lacked in inches with a big fondness for confrontation. 'Apparently Busby had been impressed when I'd got sent off with Denis Law. I think the fight we had that day might have convinced him I was what they needed when Bill Foulkes finished.'

Bill Shankly at Liverpool was never an advocate of dirty football, but he did appreciate what he had in his side. Tommy Smith recalled his manager's take on facing Everton's talented Johnny Morrissey, a player who had once been at Anfield and made the seemingly strange mistake of 'going over the top' on Smith in training. 'I thought, "I'm not having this",' Smith said. 'So I started going over the top on him. What happened in the end was that he got transferred. When we played Everton, and if John was playing, it was a tough game. Shanks would say to me, "If you get sent off, Smithy, make sure they end up with ten men as well." Which meant that I was to cripple John. But John could give it and he could take it.'

Brian Clough too, a manager who gave English football some of its most memorable and aesthetic moments, would ask much of his players, not all of it to do with football's tactics. 'We'd run out at the City ground,' says Kenny Burns. 'The opponents would be warming up and I'd hear the boss shouting over to me. "Kenneth," he'd scream. "Kenneth, the number 10 … no shin pads!" By that he meant, give him an early kick. That was the game back then.'

And with a kick, the targeted flesh could expect more than the mere leather upper of a football boot. 'It could get a bit nasty,' says Burns. 'When I was starting out, our boots had wooden studs. You had three little pins holding the studs in. What we would do is take a hacksaw and make a little cross on it, the ref would check and say fine, but then on the way out you'd whack your studs on the concrete and the pins would be sticking out. It was nasty but that was a little trick. Could cause a little cut.'

By the 1970s, football in Britain was anything but beautiful. Some had called the game 'the working man's ballet', but this was more blood in the mud. Derek Dougan, a hard forward never afraid of facing a centre-half at Wolverhampton Wanderers in the 1960s and 1970s, saw first-hand the battle between the old school and the game's reputation, even citing an upturn in crime as the fault of the national sport. 'The rough play crime-rate spiral found magistrates blaming footballers for practically everything,' he said. 'And football authorities turning round and saying that late tackles and so on were the result of a general decline in morals. Finally the authorities of football took matters into their own hands. By a sort of cloak and dagger process, a new code was brought in overnight, so that what had been permitted one season was penalised (and sometimes harshly penalised) in the next. So began a "clean up the game" campaign.'

Anyone who watched football in England in the 1970s and into the 1980s will note that the game's supposed 'clean-up' campaign was about as effective as a feather duster at a bomb site. Not to say it wasn't fun, what with maverick footballers, the likes of Stan Bowles and Frank Worthington, socks rolled down around their ankles, eyeing the pretty girl in the crowd before taking a knee-high kick from a centre-half with less amorous intentions. No, football did not clean itself up. Players did what they had to do, and were celebrated for it.

'Kenny [Burns] knew people didn't like playing against him and he'd play on that to the extent that he would threaten to volley them out if they came in our penalty box,' said Ian Bowyer, Burns' skipper at Nottingham Forest. 'You could see teams would come to our place and Larry [Lloyd] would sort one out and Kenny would sort the other out – fairly and squarely for the most part, though with Burnsy there is a very thin line between fair and unfair. But after ten minutes their strikers would be looking over their shoulders and thinking: "There's nothing for us here." I believe that first season was Burns's best year. He was made Footballer of the Year by the football writers. Can you believe it? A rogue like Burns alongside gentlemen of the game like Sir Stanley Matthews and Tom Finney. It's unbelievable.'

The 1980s, a decade of contrasts. Pristine leather Filofaxes and uncorked champagne bottles coupled with urban decay and the end of traditional industry. In football though, in terms of players using any means necessary to win games, things stayed the same. Yes, there was more TV, more scrutiny, referees said the right things about clamping down on dirty tricks and robust foul play, but put yourself in and around a penalty box at the time and you would find elbows as sharp and eager as ever, and studs as sharp and as high as they had been for the ten years before.

'I relished it,' says Leroy Rosenior, a centre-forward in the 1980s with Fulham, QPR and West Ham. 'Players accepted that there would be a degree of nastiness on the Saturday afternoon and you prepared for it, until you even came to enjoy it. You were never scared, you were ready.

'You'd gauge who you were playing and you'd brace yourself and you'd give it back. Playing against [Alan] Hansen, you know it's a footballing challenge, but there were so many that you knew wanted to leave it on you, so you thought, "OK, let's have this." I'd leave an elbow in. I'd jump for the first ball but make sure the elbow was near my head, and whack! They'd head my elbow. I was a good jumper, so leave the elbow in front of the ball, and they would make contact. You had to.

'It was protection. The likes of Kevin Moran and Eric Young, they wouldn't care, they'd look to jump and head the back of your head, never mind if they got hurt. Eric used to wear a sweatband on his head. People thought it was to keep sweat from his eyes. No chance. He was headbutting us strikers! I never saw Eric without that headband until I finished playing and he had these scarred eyebrows. All scar tissue. He'd nutted that many heads.'

Forwards like Rosenior, players who did the jumping and competing with the centre-halves, they were cannon fodder, but willingly so. Enjoying the battles, showing off the scars. The smaller strikers of the age, players like Brian Stein, Paul Walsh and Peter Beardsley, like baby zebras being tracked by lions on the African savannah, had to learn to bob and weave.

'I prefer to be marked by a big, gangly centre-half,' Peter Beardsley said while still playing. 'One that commits himself to a tackle and gives a little fellow like me the chance to nip past him. I've been lucky in that I've never been marked by out-and-out thugs. There are a few in the league, more so in the lower divisions. There are some who try to intimidate opponents by muttering things like, "I'm going to snap your legs," and similar threats.

I have a moan from time to time if I think things are getting out of hand but I'm lucky to have the temperament which means I don't react. I'm not unsettled by tough talk and I think that once your opponent resorts to that then you know you've got them worried.'

But worry could come in twos. Centre-half partnerships were vital in terms of defending, but a tag team with a reputation could intimidate the most up for it and resolute forward. 'Yeah, it was even more interesting when you had two of them enjoying the rough stuff,' says Rosenior. 'Micky Droy and Doug Rougvie at Chelsea were hard. I'd spend afternoons at Stamford Bridge bouncing off them two, but as I say, I loved giving it back. Paul Miller and Graham Roberts, they were less enjoyable, not because they were better, but they were all words. They'd try to get in your ear with the vilest comments, non-stop. Give me a straight fight every day. The two that really stand out were Malcolm Shotton and Gary Briggs. They were so dirty. Oxford had come up to the First Division from the bottom tier and those two centre-backs had no time for big names. I think their manager must have said, just kick people. And that's what they did. Every challenge was about making contact with the striker.'

And most strikers bore the scars. 'Oh don't!' yells former centre-forward Tony Cascarino at the mention of their names. 'Gary Briggs once gave me a whack – off the ball – in the face. They were notorious. Shotton never said a word. Always silent. It was quite scary. Briggs was vocal with it, but Shotton was this silent assassin. They were hugely competitive.'

Chris Waddle too winces at the mention of those two names, two players who began a reign of terror in 1985, when Oxford won promotion to the top flight. 'Oh yeah, those two were hard,' he says. 'I played up front for Tottenham at Oxford once and those two were all elbows. That's how it was back then so fine, but it could get nasty. We were away with England. Oxford had just come up and the national squad were chatting and one forward said, "Anyone played Oxford yet?" We all knew what he meant. We all agreed that these two were hard. They wouldn't last five minutes today.'

England themselves might have hoped their centre-halves had been more Shotton and Briggs in the quarter-final of the 1986 World Cup when Diego Maradona showed them the soles of his Pumas to score his second goal. Terry Butcher first, and then Terry Fenwick, who was on a booking and with a nation screaming 'Kick 'im' at their television sets, neither could. It was almost un-English of them.

So was the team's performance at the 1990 World Cup, a tournament that saw them and their central defenders, at times, look positively cultured. Terry Butcher back-heeling the ball, Mark Wright sweeping behind, Des Walker sprinting and carrying. But, this was a tournament that was far from cultured. From the first game when the wonderful Cameroon side beat Argentina, thanks largely to agricultural tackling to the last when Argentina and Germany played out the most ugly of finals, the game as a spectacle was on its knees. In England we might recall the summer of 1990 through Gazza's tears and the dulcet tones of Italian opera. In truth though, it was more argy-bargy than Pavarotti.

The governing bodies needed to take steps. Football was moving into a new, respectable, television age. The Premier League was formed in England in 1992 – not only a football league but a new money-spinning product, a global enterprise that needed to be relished for the talent on show, rather than the blood. Its cheerleaders and satellite TV cameras were new, but old habits couldn't be erased with mere razzmatazz.

Five years prior to the new era, Tottenham's Danny Thomas was tackled by Queens Park Rangers centre-half, Gavin Maguire. It was a challenge that ended Thomas' career. Maguire was to end up in court. In 1991, Gary Blissett was charged with grievous bodily harm when, while playing for Brentford, he broke the cheekbone and eye socket of Torquay defender John Uzzell. A year later, Paul Elliott, playing centre-half for Chelsea at Liverpool, suffered a career-ending injury when Dean Saunders, both feet off the ground, inflicted a 'tackle' that saw him too in a court of law. In 1993, Tottenham's centre-half, Gary Mabbutt, suffered a fractured skull after a challenge from Wimbledon's John Fashanu. Neil Ruddock at Liverpool was involved with Peter Beardsley of Newcastle, which saw the striker suffer a broken jaw. Andrew Cole at Manchester United clashed with the same Liverpool defender in a reserve game that broke the United man's ankle. Rangers' Duncan Ferguson introduced his forehead to the face of John McStay of Raith Rovers at Ibrox in 1994. Ferguson went to jail.

'I was physical and competitive but, I believed, always fair. I would never recklessly, knowingly attempt to seriously hurt any player,' says Paul Elliott, who never played again after that challenge by Dean Saunders. 'When I got seriously injured by that challenge, I didn't perceive myself as a victim. Many distinguished managers at the time and elite players said it was one of the worst two-footed challenges they had ever seen. The referee that day didn't officiate a Premier League game for the rest of that season. There are certain challenges that one consents to, which of course are within the laws of Association football. The Premier League had just been formed, so the game was constantly evolving. If the same challenge occurred now, in my view the player would receive an instant red card and suspension, as it would be deemed – at a minimum – a reckless and dangerous two-footed challenge with studs showing, which no player would consent to as it's not contained in the rules of Association Football. The rules now favour forwards. Defenders have to think, concentrate more, time their challenges and tackles to better effect. Defenders have considerably improved. The quality of the pitches with the rules yielded a better quality of players at elite level.'

Elliott's and others were all high-profile cases, not befitting the modern game, a game wanting to be so much more than just a stadium sport. Attitudes needed to change because frankly, television ratings were. Players in Europe such as Marco van Basten, the sort of player that would have people flocking to their TV sets and sponsors rushing for their wallets, had to retire from the game due to the attention his talented ankles received from over-zealous and desperate centre-halves, and that wouldn't do.

After another turgid World Cup in 1994, football needed to find its flair and so, before the 1998 World Cup in France, FIFA outlawed the 'tackle from behind', always a potent weapon for a centre-half able to let his opponent know he was around. Not anymore.

'After a terrible and cynical 1990 World Cup, FIFA needed to take action,' football writer Patrick Barclay says. 'Sepp Blatter and his adviser, Michel Platini, went to work. They called their plan Taskforce 2000 and its point was to re-engineer the game before the end of the century. The back pass rule, the offside rule, both were changed and the final and then, finally, scandalously late even, the tackle from behind was outlawed.'

Flair certainly excelled. Zinedine Zidane gracefully taking to Europe's pitches, riding, or floating over tackles yes, but now, like Ronaldinho, Alessandro Del Piero, Thierry Henry, the fear of that tackle from behind, through the back or even from the side, that was no longer a hindrance to brilliance.

And perhaps, at the game's highest level, the new rule even benefitted the centre-half. Tony Adams, for so long seen as of the old school, eager to leave a mark on a forward early on, knowing he could get away with it, became a far better player in the last quarter of his career. Much credit goes to the coaching of both Terry Venables with England and then Arsène Wenger at Arsenal and to the player himself of course, but you can make an argument for the fact that he now had to be more cultured. His game became more about intercepting rather than decapitating.

'And look at the centre-backs that became the best around,' says Patrick Barclay. 'John Terry and Jamie Carragher, for instance. Both were arguably among the best in Europe in the 2000s, getting regularly to the latter stages of the Champions League. Terry was very much a competitor, old school in as much as he wasn't the fastest and relished a battle, but he wouldn't rely on foul play, but instead his immaculate positioning. Carragher too. Carragher was probably the victim of fouls by the likes of Drogba more than he was the assailant. The modern centre-back probably makes a couple of tackles per game these days. It's midfielders who are more prone to the naughty challenge whereas your central defender has to marshal things.'

Joe Worrall agrees. 'It's true, we have to be more disciplined, which can be frustrating,' he says. 'The one position you can still really get stuck in with your tackling is at full-back. Out there they have the touchline as their guide and can still go to ground, making sliding tackles.'

It's the wingers, then, able to still get to the byline or cut in, who will be on the end of the nastier stuff in the modern game. In recent years, Crystal Palace chairman Steve Parish urged referees to protect his star asset, Wilfried Zaha. Particularly after a game at Watford that saw the player serially kicked. 'I was disappointed but not hugely surprised with his treatment at Vicarage Road, especially as Troy Deeney had previously publicly stated that his teammates take it in turns to foul him. Everyone makes tactical fouls; you can't blame them really as they are getting away with systematic fouling to help them get a result.'

Tactical fouls are coming from full-back and midfielders when the defensive lines in front of the central defenders are broken. Today the centre-half, urged to 'Stay on your feet,' told not to commit to tackles, but as the last line of defence, and with onlookers who miss the old rough and tumble of a centre-half's game, bemoaning the game as too like basketball, are there still tricks of the trade that make fans and forwards alike wince?

Not wince-inducing, but the modern centre-half can use their wiles to gain and advantage. 'First of all, we have a hundred cameras on us!' says van Dijk. 'For me personally, I don't like to hurt people. I just want to play and win fair. That's who I am. I am not a guy who will try to win with different tactics.

'Some people suggest I make the game look easy, but trust me, every game is very tough. We play against world-class strikers, very physical strikers, and never am I thinking, "This is easy." Maybe though, I want my opponent to *think* I am. Look at Roger Federer. If you see him play tennis, you think he doesn't sweat. Mentally, that must be so tough for his opponent, who will think he's not trying. Sometimes I think like that. Try to get into the head of the opponent, not by talking to him, not by kicking him, but trying to make him think that if he is going to play well or score today, he's going to have to step up. Yes, you have to be confident in your own ability, otherwise people will walk all over you and you won't be able to do what you want to do. There are other ways to win games; you don't have to kick or curse people out.'

As well as mental warfare, modern centre-halves can simply slow strikers down, taking them off route by leaning on them and using a weight advantage. Again it might lack the crunching barbarity of years gone by, but it is effective in this non-contact version of the game. Shirt pulling and using the arm to hinder the run of a striker are also both cleverly used. 'I guess there are not so many dirty players anymore but there are still dark arts – look at Sergio Ramos, he's the master,' says Joe Worrall. 'Most of it though is trying to con the ref. I won't name names but we have players at Forest who will throw themselves to the ground in training. It can be a bugbear but at the end of the day, if any of our attackers go down easily but win us a penalty then happy days. On the flip side, I can't grumble when it goes against us. I don't condone cheating, but it is becoming part of the game and if it goes against you, why not to try to utilise it too? I would never go on to a pitch and try to hurt someone. You get people standing on your foot when you try to jump, but not a lot. The new one is pushing the opponent into the advertising hoardings. You'll see it a lot. Your opponent is running at pace to keep the ball in play, and you give a gentle shove in the back, and into the billboards. I've had it done to me too.'

It's a ploy long employed by over-zealous centre-halves. 'Oh yeah, I hated that one,' says Tony Cascarino. 'I hated it more than the dreaded tackle from behind. I could handle that one. No, the one I hated was when the ball was played into the channel, you'd make the run and the centre-half would deliberately time his tackle to put you in the stands. Honestly that was so commonplace, it would happen two or three times in a game. Graham Roberts and Paul Miller loved that one. They'd give you half a yard and then bang, you're on a fan's lap in Row 3. It was like Aussie Rules football in the 70s and 80s.'

So today, on beautiful pitches, in beautiful stadia, with VAR cameras and the public's morals heavily scrutinising the game and those who play it, has the game suffered for its new lack of physicality? Paul Elliott, a player whose career was cut short by that physicality, ponders the point. 'That's a good question,' he says. 'I still love the Championship. It reigns supreme with the competitive balance, and is so exciting to watch. It's such an authentic league that has retained its integrity, those crunching challenges that set the tone for a game. The game has evolved so positively in the Premier League as it's a global brand but, like many current, ex-pros and analysts players feigning injury and getting players booked and sent off is so unpalatable and unsporting.'

Yes, the dark arts are still with us. They just no longer leave bruises.

8

'THAT TYPE OF SAMBA ...'

The South Americans

A South American centre-half. Doesn't sound quite right, does it? Not to those with a party to go to. It is like the moody security man at the party of the year, or the caterer on an adult film set. Kind of important, but not the reason for anyone being there. It doesn't look right and it certainly isn't part of the fun. To some, the position on this flair-driven corner of the world is a footballing oxymoron, a blasphemy on the game's romantic notions. Why would anyone want to stop a goooooooooaaaaaal?

Sat between two raging oceans, South America is a continent taking it from all sides. It took football primarily from British settlers, but in time, they took the game, manipulated it, adapted it, brought it into line with their own physicality, and, like Indians picking up English cricket bats in the seventeenth century, made it somehow so much better.

But where do central defenders fit in? After all, you don't see many lithe, beautiful, tanned locals launching headers or showing off their sliding tackles on Copacabana Beach. Don't be fooled though. While carnival and colour and the samba and the tango are easily brought to mind when we think about the football there, the South American spirit, an underdog growl that won't be tamed, is one that sees their teams cross the white line with a will to win that even the best party can't subside. The South American centre-half then, while for so long trying to find their way in a new way of playing the game, has been as vital to the success, and even the romance brought to the global game by this amazing continent.

Not that they can always be celebrated like their dancing cousins up front. In Argentina, two players have lifted the World Cup trophy above their heads. Two very different players. In 1986, Diego Maradona, a footballer making a case for expanding the competition to further parts of the universe, succeeded Daniel Passarella, who had got his hands on the golden trophy in Buenos Aires in 1978.

The latter is regarded as one of the best defenders the game has produced. A Franz Beckenbauer with an Argentine twist. 'El Kaiser' was a suitable nickname. A brilliant captain, but less loved in Argentina than Maradona. No shame in that, of course, but there is an argument that his rigidity and strait-laced approach (perhaps akin to the position he played) has links to the military dictator Jorge Videla, while Maradona, and those hips that moved as if looking for a lover on the streets of his capital's San Telmo district, spoke to the people and their passions far more eloquently. Perhaps centre-halves have always, anywhere in the world, struggled to connect with the people as easily as those with romantic attacking intent, it's just that in South America, the differences have long been felt more keenly. It's just part of the DNA.

Take Brazil, a country used to having its culture of dance, martial arts, and carnival brought into the conversations about their football. In *Inverting the Pyramid*, Jonathan Wilson quotes the anthropologist Roberto DaMatta, who spoke of a theory he called, '*Jeitinho*' or 'the small way' explaining why Brazilians take such pride in being creative, as a means of simply getting by. '*Jetinho,*' wrote DaMatta, 'is a personal mediation between the law, the situation in which it should apply and the persons involved in such a way that nothing really changes, apart from a considerable demoralisation of the law itself … In the USA, France and England, for example, the rules are either obeyed or do not exist. In these societies, it is well known that there is no desire to establish new laws that are not in line with the common good or with the other laws of society, so creating room for bureaucratic corruption and diminishing the trust in the public institutions … So … the Americans, the French and the British stop in front of a "Stop" sign, which seems to us a logical and social absurdity.'

In short, and in relation to our central defenders, Brazilians like to go around a stop sign, not be one. Wilson goes on to say, 'Brazilians … find a way around such restrictions; they come to rely on themselves rather than on the external structures. It is not hard to see the imaginativeness that has historically characterised Brazilian football as a particular expression of that trait. Individuals find their own way to master situations, and that means both high levels of creativity, and a distrust of teamwork.'

Football had come to Brazil with an Englishman named Charles Miller. Having been educated in England, Miller arrived back in Brazil to his English father and Brazilian mother in 1894 and in time a thriving scene had spread from the cricket clubs of São Paulo to Rio de Janeiro, and while authority and systems were to be mistrusted (naturally), skills and a way of doing things began to stand out.

One of the great Brazilian players of the 1930s was Domingos da Guia. A defender. His style of play – skilful, with a penchant for rhythmic dribbling from defence – might have had the doyens of the three-back system in Britain at the time hiding behind their tactical clipboards, but it symbolised a very Brazilian way of seeing defence. 'When I was still a kid I was scared to play football,' da Guia said, 'because I often saw black players ... get whacked on the pitch, just because they made a foul or sometimes for less than that ... My elder brother used to tell me: the cat always falls on his feet. Aren't you good at dancing? I was and this helped my football. I swung my hips a lot. That short dribble I invented imitating *miudinho*, that type of samba.'

The Argentines and – even more so – the Uruguayans had grasped the tactical, systematic nature of football faster than the more gyrating Brazilians. Uruguay won the inaugural World Cup in 1930, preceded by two Olympic golds in 1924 and 1928, and they won the World Cup again in 1950, in Rio de Janeiro, causing a period of mourning in a country that would find it hard to forgive those who had played. Especially those pesky defenders.

Brazil had scored twenty-two goals in the six games, but the two conceded in the final would hold a nation's attention for decades to come. Uruguay's Obdulio Varela marshalled a back-line ultimately frustrating the Brazilian forwards and nation itself, while the more free-flowing Juvenal at the heart of Brazil's back three was susceptible, and the whole back-line deemed culpable.

Barbosa, the goalkeeper, too. The story goes that twenty years after the final, he was in a shop when a woman pointed to him and said to her young son, 'Look at him, he's the man who made all of Brazil cry.' Later he would say, 'In Brazil, the maximum sentence is thirty years, but I have served fifty.'

For the next World Cup, Juvenal would be replaced by the more defensive Pinheiro as the nation started the process of coupling their brand of creative football with a more reliable defensive system. Perhaps some romance was in jeopardy but they still managed to avoid the rigidness of the WM formation. In his 1953 book, *Soccer: The World Game*, Geoffrey Green wrote of the Latin game, that, '[They] have so much to teach us, and those who say that they and others on the Continent, by sticking to a roving centre-half, and by remaining ball artists are twenty-five years behind the times are talking absolute nonsense.'

Green was clinging to the hope that a back-line could be fluid, writing his book in a year when the game's tectonic plates were shifting and the tsunami of Hungarian play had changed English perceptions of themselves and a game ever-changing. Brazil would make their own tactical changes but that idea that a brilliant attacking side can be let down by those at the back wouldn't subside. Three decades later, in Spain, Brazil's wonderfully adventurous team at the 1982 World Cup came unstuck and once again, those centre-halves were to blame.

Oscar was a talented player at centre-half with an eye for stepping forward, and was partnered by Luizinho, an equally talented player. The latter was remarkably named the best centre-half in the tournament but with Socrates, Zico, Falcão and Cerezo in midfield it was widely thought that such talent was let down by others. The sizzling 3–2 defeat to Italy that saw them eliminated was a pure example of Brazil's *jojo bonito* (the beautiful game) being let down by boring pedantic duties such as defending. Brian Glanville wrote that it was, 'The game in which Brazil's glorious midfield, put finally to the test, could not make up for the deficiencies behind and in front of it.'

Truth is it was Cerezo's error in midfield that gifted Paolo Rossi the second of his three goals and the whole team, that midfield included, were far too open at 2–2, when a draw would have sufficed to send them to the semi-finals.

There was, of course, romance in defeat. This is Brazil. The centre-half, Oscar said of people who suggest that history is written by winners: 'They are wrong. It's like our feet heard music, and they danced to a beat.' The only problem being such was the concern with a lack of balance in the nation's play that after Spain, that tune had to be changed. Luizinho certainly reflected on what might have been. 'If we had won playing our way,' he said, 'there would have been no reason for the '94 team to abandon *jogo bonito*.'

That inherent mistrust of a stop sign, even if it is your own, was going to change. By 1994, when Brazil reclaimed their global crown, they had adhered to a more solid style of play. Many of their players earned their corn in Europe, so that continent took a lot of the blame from those missing a hitherto carnival style of play, but at centre-half they had adopted players with a firm will to win, tantamount to other parts of South America.

Aldair, the linchpin of the Brazilian side in 1994 and beyond, was one of the finest defenders South America or anywhere has produced. Big, strong, dependable, talented. After what had come before, it was the dependable that stuck out, but it was also a lean towards genuine holding midfielders such as the captain, Dunga, that truly shored things up. After all, World Cup winning teams in 1958, 1962 and 1970 had had more than talented centre-halves. Bellini in '58, a solid leader who invented the act of lifting a trophy above the head, Mauro in '62, a fantastically uncompromising but cerebral defender who once said of a team ethic, 'Each of us has a theoretical zone of action, a sort of anchorage. But it is a starting point, not the finish. [Each player's] real scope of action is dictated by his own reading of the match, and his self-knowledge of his skill and physical possibilities.'

Then there were Brito and Piazza in the 1970 ensemble, not the last lines of defence, just *the* lines of defence in a wonderfully forward-thinking side. Piazza was actually a midfielder and such was the manager Mário Zagallo's desire to keep the ball, he had him play centre-half where he could start things off and it was he who dispatched the ball to Clodoaldo in midfield, whose high jinks started the move for Carlos Alberto's unforgettable fourth goal in the final.

But with holding midfielders raised to do that job, not asked to, Brazil and their centre-halves by the mid-1990s were far more akin to the more pragmatic corners of their continent. Uruguay's José Nasazzi, and then Obdulio Varela, defensive players with a team's safety at heart. The same nation gave us Paolo Montero, the Juventus centre-half who took personal umbrage to the idea of a forward getting past him; and more recently, Diego Godin, a brilliantly competitive defender, who like his predecessors would sell parts of his own body before giving up space, let alone goals.

Godin, at Atlético Madrid, coached by an Argentine terrier in Diego Simeone, the two of them symbolic of their two countries' desire to take anything on, and the La Liga they won together by triumphing over Real Madrid and Barcelona was a mastery in suffocating defence and quick-fire counter-attack. Godin was key. His refusal to follow the Guardiola school of aesthetic defending in as much as how they manipulated the ball in possession, and focus on his raw desire to defend, yes, defend, block, cover, or as the *Independent* put it, 'It was why Godin stood out all the more. He gave attackers a problem they just struggled to deal with it. That may have made something of a throwback, but also ensured he was for a long time the very best centre-half in the world.'

Montero, too, all Uruguayan brimstone, with a look to an opposing forward warming up that would suggest the poor fellow's ankles were about to have a hard time. He had arrived in Italy with Atalanta, managed by Marcello Lippi, and when the great coach took over at Juventus and wanting steel to protect the talent he had up top, Montero received the call.

Playing next to Ciro Ferrara and behind Didier Deschamps, who held midfields as if they were his children, Montero was part of a brilliant, multi-*scudetto*-winning team. He was ultra-competitive; not the tallest, but seemingly with the sort of small man syndrome that had him out-jump buildings. He was a good player. But he was a dirty player. To Paolo Montero, the tackle from behind – no, the crunch from behind – was an art. Sixteen red cards in twelve seasons in Italy are a colourful reminder of his style, and the colour of the mist that descended whenever there was a ball to be won and a striker to be maimed.

Reputations are thus made. Not only individual ones, but those of a country and even a continent. South American defenders were long looked upon with suspicion, especially by the more pure European coaches, who as they started to play against them more regularly held them in contempt, seeing them like a father might see their teenage daughter's new boyfriend.

In the 1966 World Cup quarter-final when England beat Argentina, the villain of the piece was Antonio Rattin, sent off and refusing to go. In Jack Charlton's autobiography, he described Rattin as 'Argentina's centre-half'. He was a midfielder. Maybe an honest mistake or maybe a simple prejudice that such behaviour from a South American must come from those at the back.

Such thoughts had petrol thrown upon them a year later when European Champions, Celtic, faced Racing Club of Argentina and champions of South America in the World Club Championship. Jock Stein left Uruguay (the tie went to a third match on 'neutral' ground after it finished level over two legs) saying, 'I would not bring a team to South America again for all the money in the world,' after three games that saw spitting, kicking, punching, a bit of verbal abuse and outright brawling. In the third game that saw Racing Club win 1–0, six players were sent off, four of them Scottish, but for retaliating to what was eager and consistent baiting. The Racing Club centre-half, Alfio Basile, was given a red, affirming those sentiments towards defenders from those parts.

But let us not dwell on stereotypes and prejudices. Plenty of the centre-half fraternity from all corners of the world have enjoyed those nastier sides to the game but there can also be beauty and honour. After the game and amid riotous scenes (the Uruguayan crowd had followed the players lead in violent conduct) Billy McNeill approached Racing's Roberto Perfumo.

Perfumo was a stylish sweeper for the national team who had played right-back that night, and expected the Celt to be looking for some afters.

Instead, a large but honest Scottish hand was offered and their shirts were exchanged. Perfumo hugged McNeill and said in Spanish, 'This is how football should be played.' McNeill in a Lanarkshire form of Perfumo's language said, '*Buena suerte, buena suerte*' ('Good luck, good luck'). It was a flower of sportsmanship among the weeds of brutality.

So let's concentrate on the flowers of South America, a place that has provided so much joy to the world of football, even from centre-half. Daniel Passarella was both flower and weed. A dandelion, with the emphasis on lion. As Argentina captain, he ruled the roost. Steely, almost militaristic in his organisation of men, Passarella was all guile on the ball, perfectly suited for his position, and while Mario Kempes' goals won the country their first World Cup in 1978, it was the centre-half's ability as sweeper that controlled games and (arguably with the assistance of some more than dodgy decisions) ultimately won the tournament.

He would be succeeded two decades later as Argentine captain by Roberto Ayala. A wonderful footballing centre-half more in line with the game in the 1990s, where rules were changing and an emphasis shifted from brute to cute. Having said that the man from Paraná recently seemed disheartened by the modern version of his position, saying that thanks largely to those wanting to follow Guardiola's lead, the position had become too self-indulgent, too keen to impress. 'In a way, it has damaged football,' he said. 'Now many defenders want to play the ball out as if they were in Barcelona, and they're not able to.

They're not centre midfielders. First of all you have to defend, to give security. You can't lose sight of the fact that they are defenders first.'

Ayala could do both and excelled in both Spain and Italy, winning the La Liga with Valencia in 2000/01, playing at a time when the South American centre-half was the most sought after around. An ageing Aldair had helped Roma to a *scudetto* in the same year Ayala triumphed in Spain, and then in 2002, the Brazilian Lucio helped Brazil win the World Cup in Japan. Part of a back three offering a wall of knowing defiance and allowing the full-backs, Cafu and Roberto Carlos, licence to put the miles in.

Lucio was a great talent, Brazilian in every part of his nature and game, never afraid to move forward with the ball, but never forgetting that events behind him were always of the utmost importance. At club level he won trophies in Germany before helping José Mourinho's Internazionale win the Treble in 2010.

And then, into the noughties, his countryman Thiago Silva continued his work, delighting Europe with similar gusto, swatting away attacks one minute, stepping out to start them the next. Modern, exhilarating, and very South American. Have we then forgotten about previous cynicism about Brazilian and even South American centre-halves? Don't be too sure.

David Luiz today invites much ridicule, a lot of it unfair, a lot of it not. A string of mistakes against Manchester City in Arsenal's first game back after the Covid lockdown in 2020 brought nothing but scorn from those in England unable to comprehend him as a centre-half. Clearly talented, clearly able to do much with a football, a man (like his hair) full of joyous bounce – but doubts, especially in England, remain about whether he is up to the more pragmatic aspects of his job.

Perhaps it all links back to DaMatta, our anthropologist who deemed the Brazilian psyche inherently unable to follow instruction or basic laws. Why should Luiz conform? Or maybe it's simpler. 'The thing is,' says former Liverpool defender, Mark Lawrenson, 'to be a centre-back, you have to be a pessimist. That David Luiz, great player, but he ain't a pessimist, is he?' No, he's South American.

9

'NO FRIENDS ON THE PARK, SON'

The Epic Battle between Centre-Half and Centre-Forward

Leroy Rosenior doesn't need a second thought. When asked what comes to mind when he's greeted with the words, 'centre-half', two words quickly spring from the memory banks: 'Tony Adams.' Rosenior was an elegant centre-forward who plied his trade in the 1980s and 1990s, scoring goals for – among others – Fulham, Queens Park Rangers and West Ham. A physical target man with finesse, good on the ball, a fine finisher and able to hang in the air like a cloud with attitude, he knew a thing or two about the battles long fought between forwards and defenders of the central variety.

'Tony Adams was the best I ever played against,' Rosenior continues, a revelation that should come as no surprise. 'Ask most of the forwards who played in the late 1980s and into the Nineties and I reckon most of them would agree.' Again, fair enough, not many got the better of the Arsenal captain. No, it's the reason Rosenior gives that says so much about the nature of the battle on the pitch that can so define a match. 'The thing about Tony was you never knew where he was.'

There is a wide belief that a centre-half would always want the forward to know where he was. 'Let him know you're fuckin' there,' is after all a particular battle cry in the almost biblical tussles between the two positions, but Adams, early in his career too often dismissed as nothing but a bruiser, understood the more subtle arts of shadowing his striking opponent.

'Don't get me wrong,' Rosenior continues, 'Tony could get touch tight, sure he'd love to mix it with you but he had this other, clever side to his game where he would avoid contact. You'd be grappling with your arms behind you, hoping to get a sense of where he was, wanting to use his body as a pivot to roll him, or hold the ball up against, but nothing and it was very disconcerting, and then, just as you were working out your next move, a leg would appear and he was nicking the ball away from you and your attack was over. Very clever and very, very good.'

Cat and mouse? No. Lion and gazelle? Not really. The relationship between the centre-half and his centre-forward foe has long been one of equals. Whether it's using brute strength, sheer nastiness or Tony Adams' elusive guile, the contest has been a vital one and when you talk to those who took to either role at any level, there is always respect.

Well, almost always. 'Big, ugly, spoilers, guys who didn't have any skill, but enjoy being destructive' is former Crystal Palace and Sheffield Wednesday striker Mark Bright's assessment of those tasked with marking him during his playing days but overall, however many knocks, broken noses, limbs and broken pride, the two seem to have lived a fascinatingly competitive existence. Side by side, toe to toe, back to front, one on top of the other.

Today, a far more psychological warfare is played out. Those at the top of the game are forced to rely on slyness of thought rather than the sly dig of an elbow. 'Growing up playing on the streets in the Netherlands, I learnt a few things that developed my mindset about how strikers think,' says Virgil van Dijk. 'It sounds a bit easy, but I know a striker loves to have a defender make the decision for him. A striker can then act on instinct.

'What I like to do is make the striker do the thinking. Let him think, think, think. I have spoken to plenty of strikers – teammates – and I know it is difficult for them if they aren't given an option. If you are stepping in with your left, he can take it to your right and so on. If you wait and hold, and you give him a trap that he can run into, then he can overthink and the chance is missed.'

Prior to the stopper centre-half in the 1920s, the two rarely met. Not until the WM formation pushed the centre-half backwards, like Hollywood's Terminator sent back in time to destroy a centre-forward's fun, did the two begin to get to know one another. And immediately there were clashes, clashes that would seemingly last a lifetime.

Dixie Dean, that swashbuckling centre-forward who was first at Tranmere and then most impressively at Everton in the 1920s and 1930s, was known for his civility on the field, but that didn't put centre-halves off acquainting themselves with any body part whose heavy bruising might save their afternoon from heavy defeat. He told the *Liverpool Echo*:

I'd just broken into the first team at Tranmere and had scored two first-half goals to put us 2–0 up at half-time. Halfway through the second half, Rochdale's centre-half sidled up to me and told me in no uncertain terms that my goalscoring exploits had finished for the day. I took no notice of him and carried on with the game. A few minutes later, however, a kick to the genitals laid me out flat. In an attempt to ease the pain, one of my teammates began to rub them. 'Never mind bloody rubbing them – count them!' I shouted. I ended up in hospital that night. It was my first taste of the rough stuff that I would have to put up with for the rest of my career.

The rough stuff. That was now the norm. Stopper centre-halves tasked with doing it by any means necessary. Dean himself was known for the restraint and even humour he showed under close scrutiny. Joe Mercer, himself a great of the English pre- and post-war game, saw Dean's ability to not give it back to central-defenders as a major asset. 'Dixie Dean's greatest secret was that he would never retaliate,' said Mercer. 'They would push him out, he would stand there. If he'd pockets in his shorts he would have put his hands in them. But when he moved, a goal was on the way.'

Matt Busby agreed. '[Dean] put your heart in your boots every time he had the ball, but he was a great sportsman and was never nasty. He took a terrific hammering, we were all trying to cut him down, but I never knew him to moan or retaliate.'

So the word 'retaliate' is used frequently, but let's not paint these goal-seeking centre-forwards as mere shrinking violets, damsels in distress, chased by evil dragons as they try to simply make their way to the penalty area's shiny kingdom. Centre-halves would have to learn to take it too.

Stan Cullis, a cerebral centre-half for Wolverhampton Wanderers and England before the war, talking in the 1960s, had no doubt about how much more physical the game was when he laced his boots. 'It was more rugged,' he said. 'There was more physical contact. We always had what we called the killers in the game, players who went deliberately over the ball, to get the man. They were all known and you took precautions against them. The play was rougher and dirtier than it is now.'

And if it wasn't the forwards' studs making themselves known to your shins, then his tongue might attack your ears. The relationship between centre-half and centre-forward, even back in those jolly nice Pathé news days, was verbal as well as physical. For centre-forwards such as Scotland's diminutive but destructive Hughie Gallacher, the mouth was often his best weapon. 'Hughie was always talking, arguing, and swearing to rile the opposition,' said Bill Shankly of his fellow countryman years later. 'He would say to big centre-halves, "How did you get on the field? You won't get a kick of the ball today!" Everybody would be chasing him, trying to kill him!'

Again Matt Busby concurs. 'Gallacher seemed unrobbable,' he said of his fellow Lanarkshire native's ability to keep the ball, even under the attack of the most nasty of defenders. 'If the ball had been tied to his boots with string it could not have been more adhesive. Incidentally, Gallacher took as much stick from tough nut defenders as any modern "great" does. I saw the bruises.'

That was (and is) the thing. Centre-forwards have long seen themselves as superior to their defending counterparts. They are there to bring glory. Their opponents are there to stop it. And for so long it seems, defenders had to live with that inferiority complex, relying only on those 'tough nut' tendencies, but humbled when faced with greatness.

There were none much better at the art of goalscoring than Tommy Lawton. A centre-parted, Brylcreemed, *Boy's Own* hero, who relished the challenge set by those asked to stop him. Lawton said: 'I always remember a bloke called Syd Bycroft who played for Doncaster Rovers. He was 6 foot 3, raw-boned, couldn't play, thick as two planks, and it's like he used to say to me, "I can't play and you're not going to." I was the England centre-forward when Everton were drawn against Doncaster Rovers in the Cup, and this Bycroft knocked on our dressing-room door, opened it, and said, "Is this Lawton playing?"

'Little Alex Stevenson says, "Yeah, why?"

'"Where is he?" he says.

'Alex said, "You'll see enough of him when you get on the park. You'll see the back of him. Close the door on your way out."

'This was Stevie, you know, he was quick. "Run him ragged," he said to me. "Run him ragged today." I got four, and we licked them 8–0.'

And forwards wonder why they get kicked! Harold Atkinson, a less gifted striker than Lawton (and there is no shame in that), recalled his own run-in while playing for Tranmere just after the war: 'I always remember the first game I played at Wrexham and there was a centre-half called Bill Tudor. Bill had legs bigger than me. He was massive. He used to head the ball further than I could kick it. He came up to me and said, "Get past me, and I'll break both your legs." I just looked at him. I was *giving* him the ball.'

But as the post-war game developed, central-defending became that bit more refined. Yes, they were there to stop, yes, a centre-forward could expect oak-like legs to be in his wooded path to goal, but plenty more players were becoming more like Stan Cullis' thoughtful version of the role, rather than Bill Tudor, seemingly as subtle as Henry VIII with a drumstick when it came to the defensive arts.

No longer did a player have to be one or the other. Ron Greenwood (and it's interesting that both he and Stan Cullis as centre-halves who thought of doing more than merely 'Stopping' went on to become two of this country's most innovative coaches) was an early advocate of doing things another way. Taking the fight to the forward's brain as well as his ankles.

'I was not a battling centre-half,' he says in Jim Holden's biography, *Stan Cullis: The Iron Manager*, 'although I was ready to tackle hard: the ability to mix it is often essential. Basically, though, I avoided contact for the sake of it … I was more concerned with the ball than with my opponents. I tried to read the game intelligently, holding back to mark space rather than a man, to win the ball by thinking first and moving first. My game was all about anticipation.'

Greenwood could be describing the modern centre-half and he wasn't alone. Nat Lofthouse, the big-limbed and big-hearted Bolton and England centre-forward, wrote in his book, *Goals Galore*, of those foes who could get the better of him: 'There were three in particular who always gave me a hard time: Stan Cullis of Wolves and Neil Franklin of Stoke and Manchester City's Dave Ewing. I could always understand my problems with Franklin and Cullis. They were clever players, read the game well. They seemed to be one step ahead of me all the time.'

Interestingly, Lofthouse is more pained by the physical Ewing, almost ashamed to be outmuscled, proving that the rough stuff was far from leaving the game. 'Dave was different. He was a big man, a pure stopper. And when you ran into Big Dave you stopped! Every time we played City I'd say, "I've got to beat this devil today." But I never did. I'd play like a real donkey. Dave always came out on top.'

Alan Shearer, very much in the Lofthouse class of physical specimen, had one run-in with his former club teammate Colin Hendry when England faced Scotland in the European Championship play-off in 1999. 'I knew Alan's game,' says Hendry. 'That's not to say I was going to get the better of him and so I made the decision to test him early. I went right through him early on. I got booked but I thought, "Let's see how he copes," and from there, Alan was actually quite quiet. I actually used to do well against him. The only goal he got was quite important; the first in the 2–0 win against us at Wembley during Euro '96.'

And so to modernity. As footballers' shorts became shorter, their lives became more glamorous, and their clothes more finely cut. Talking of glamour, in 1958, Billy Wright, England's captain, and now centre-half, married one-third of the Beverley Sisters (think Posh Spice marrying Tony Adams) and with such niceties came new tactics, new responsibilities, new challenges.

The FA's Official Yearbook for the 1960/61 season contained an essay asking, 'How Can the Block Defence be Penetrated?' It posed tactical questions about how forward lines should best get the better of packed defences, underlining how the game was changing and how it was no longer simply about a winger beating a full-back and a centre-forward nodding the ball home.

'A simple twofold purpose underlies any game of football,' it starts, wonderfully setting out the purpose of this very chapter.

'To score goals and to prevent them being scored.' It went on to argue with charm that it was easier to score if the final pass was closer to goal than further away, which may seem obvious but the fact that it spoke of the need for new and intricate approach play speaks volumes of newer thoughts. 'Even so, it is often possible to play the ball towards the strongest section of the defensive block, and by means of a quick return pass or deflection to give another attacker a brief moment in which to shoot at goal from an unexpected angle. While this may seem to call for a high degree of skill, it is not as difficult as it appears and the understanding that is developed by constant practice of such tight approach play can bring about a vast improvement in performance.'

Yes, minds were expanding and questions would have to be answered. Centre-halves and now their central defensive partners had to deal with so much more than merely stopping the big man up front. Full-backs such as Jimmy Armfield had started to bomb on, overlapping their wide men, asking centre-halves to move from side to side, as well as just looking ahead. The blinkers were off.

In *The Soccer Syndrome*, John Moynihan describes the then current England centre-half Jack Charlton, saying, 'He plays a spherical game on a line lapping both penalty spots and the flags on the halfway line. He roars around this circle like a speedway rider, in turn mopping up rival attacks and coming to the other end, often via the wings, to attack the opposing goal or take a thrusting header.'

Charlton himself would concur, himself describing a time when he dealt with the threat of an ageing but still brilliant winger, Stanley Matthews, early in his career, underlining that the centre-half was now being asked to look after the wingers as well as the centre-forwards. 'I was twenty,' he said. '[Matthews] was forty. He was like greased lightning. The only way I could get to him was by grabbing his shirt. Stanley stopped the ball dead and turned to me and said, "Why did you feel you had to do that, son?" I felt so ashamed and such a twit. All I could say was, "I am very sorry, Mr Matthews." He gave me a withering look, and was off again with the ball like quicksilver.'

Charlton's shame wouldn't stop him getting at forwards for the rest of his illustrious career but the dye was set. Skilful threats would now come from all over the pitch and the centre-half had better get used to it. For now he had to deal with not only a bruising centre-forward but also tricky and annoyingly skilful sidekicks.

Andrew Cole, that most lithe and lively of centre-forwards, who excelled in the 1990s and 2000s with Newcastle and Manchester United (among others), is deadpan when asked about those sturdy fellows asked to stop him. 'They were my opponent,' he says. 'That was all, and that's how I approached them. They were the men I had to beat, the men I had to get the better of if I was to benefit my team.'

But what of individuals? But what about preparing for specific challenges, for specific opponents? 'Are you kidding?' says Cole. 'I never once thought of the individual I was going to face at the weekend. My thoughts were all about my game. Yes, I faced some great centre-halves. Tony Adams, Sol Campbell, Colin Hendry, even the greats at Juventus such as Ciro Ferrara, but that never bothered me. I wanted to test myself against the best and of course it was always tough but I loved working on my strengths and hoping that was enough to help my team win a game of football.'

Cole played at a time when centre-forwards had to cope with brute strength, referees were still lax when it came to the first few challenges – however strong – being, shall we say missed, but what Cole lacked in any old school definition of physicality he made up for in craft and action, and ask most centre-halves, they would prefer a street fight rather than a fox hunt.

'My whole game was about trying my best to deceive the centre-half. My game had that. I was a good finisher but most forwards are, but my movement was my strength and what I loved to do was try to mess a centre-half about. Always mess them about.

'Everything I did was to play opposites. By that, I mean if the defender wanted to step up, fine, I'll run the angle, if he wants to drop off, I'll go deeper. You have to get under these guys' skins and try to upset people.'

Centre-halves can be easily upset. Ask would they rather face that Cole-like deception, or a big man with sharp elbows, and most would offer to bring a sharpening file; even the most competent could be upset by guile over brawn. 'The guy who gave me the most cuts was John Fashanu,' says Tony Adams. 'But ask me who gave me more problems football-wise and it was the No.10s. Beardsley, Sheringham, Zidane, Maradona, Bergkamp and Dalglish. Those types. What I did was start a little black book regarding all my opponents so I knew how to play them all. I relished all the styles I faced.'

Alan Reeves, Wimbledon's centre-half in the mid-1990s, has no doubt. 'Oh, give me the big guy anytime,' he says. 'I remember playing Sheffield Wednesday once and Chris Waddle was up front with Mark Bright. Waddle was about thirty-three by then but was doing those step overs of his and left me behind a couple of times.

That bloody shimmy of his. I thought, "Christ, this is going to be a long afternoon. First fifteen minutes he's left me twice."

'Kenny Cunningham, a good, mobile player, was centre-back with me that day and marking Brighty, who was great in the air and was doing Kenny each time. "Fancy swapping with me?" Kenny asked and I didn't hesitate. We won 1–0.'

Clive Allen, a top striker reliant on his pace, brain and finishing prowess in the 1980s, had to find ways to overcome his opponents without the gift of brawn, and the fact that he scored 47 goals in one season while playing alone up front in an innovative 4-5-1 formation in the 1986/87 season proves that his skills in the regard were finely tuned. 'You learnt quickly to deal with intimidation,' he says. 'They wanted to scare you. Centre-halves liked to make their mark, in more ways than one, as my young ankles could testify, but you learnt to combat it by asking them questions. They don't like that.

'A lot of it for us smaller players is about working the angles, upsetting the centre-halves by shifting them from their comfort zones, and making runs in behind. When I played up front alone, I would try to work the spaces between the two defenders. Nothing riles them more than being elusive, being mobile and by asking questions of them that don't involve simply the rough stuff.'

But enough of such technicalities – let's address the rough stuff. In a sport where stadiums are still referred to as *theatres* or *coliseums*, we must talk more of the sheer drama and bloodshed that can happen when centre-forwards pull their swords and centre-halves wield their shields.

'That's it, it was a battle,' says Mick Hartford, a centre-forward from the 1980s and 1990s whose combination of talent and aggression had centre-backs everywhere asking for a bonus after facing him. 'On a Friday you were preparing for battle. I used to see it as a game within a game. Two v two. Me and my strike partner against the two centre-backs.

'My focus was on looking after my strike partner, who was usually smaller. Brian Stein, for instance. I had to make sure he was all right because I knew the likes of Steiney, a brilliant footballer, but he was going to be targeted by two louts.'

Even today, in these less loutish times, centre-halves will also focus on the striker or strikers they must stop if their team is to prevail. Steph Houghton, Manchester City and England's centre-half, mirrors Hartford's take. 'Yes, I see it as game within a game,' she says. 'In the bigger games I very much focus on a centre-forward and think if I can stop her then my team has a great chance. You need to know their strengths and what type of movement they enjoy, and I prepare for that. It's important to win your one v one battle and if I win mine at centre-half, then the team has a great chance.'

Clive Allen realised from a young age that the two men paid to stop him were far from the cuddly type, even if they were family friends. 'When I joined the Queens Park Rangers playing staff, the kids would play the first team,' he says. 'Now my dad, Les, had played for the club and was good mates with Dave Webb and his centre-half partner, Frank McLintock.

'I had grown up with Dave, who was especially close to Dad, but as soon as the game started, I got a taste for how, how shall we put this?, How professional they were. No quarters were given and they made me fully aware that I was merely a young upstart. I was sitting on my backside very early in that game. I saw it as an initiation.'

For Leroy Rosenior, the challenge faced came in two parts. 'It could be a footballing challenge, when you faced the likes of Alan Hansen at Liverpool or, as I say, Tony Adams at Arsenal, but usually it was a physical challenge. Sometimes it was both. At Arsenal, Tony would play that non-contact game when he wanted to. Clever stuff. But alongside him was Martin Keown. He'd send shivers down the spine. A psychopath. Martin was a good player but he had these shark eyes and you didn't know what was going to happen next.' Not that Rosenior was ever scared. 'You were never terrified, no. You had to be ready though.'

On one occasion, though, as a young centre-forward playing for Fulham in the old Second Division, Rosenior was far from ready for a horror moment in the dressing room and the seemingly murderous intent of an opposing centre-half called Sam Allardyce. 'We were playing at Huddersfield,' recalls Rosenior. 'Jeff Hopkins was a lovely fella but he mistimed a tackle and broke the opponent's leg. Crack. It was horrible. Jeff was ashen-faced and amid uproar, he was sent back to the dressing room. Allardyce was playing and wanted revenge. You could see it in his eyes.

'Towards the end of the game, I went off injured, and was sitting in the dressing room with a crestfallen Jeff, when suddenly a fist came through the door. A fist! It belonged to Big Sam and it was like something from a horror film. Jeff and I scrambled into the showers as Sam was pulled away, by about twenty men!'

While nothing can prepare a centre-forward for the image of big Sam Allardyce, like Jack Nicholson in *The Shining* ('Here's Saaammmmmmmy!') smashing through doors, the likes of Mick Hartford soon learnt to give as good as they got. 'It was all about intimidation,' says Hartford. 'They wanted to intimidate us forwards and I soon decided that I should just do the same back.'

Hartford's teammate at Wimbledon, Alan Reeves, recalls a clash at Highbury when the centre-forward decided to take steps to harpoon Keown's shark eyes. 'Martin had been putting it about a bit. We got a corner and Martin was zonal at the front post. I usually made the run there, but Mick gave me this look, as if to say, I'm going there. Off he goes and as the ball flies over both him and Martin, Mick puts a headbutt on him. Bang! It was premeditated and Martin was out. Play on. Words were said, and in the tight tunnel at half-time, Mick had Martin up against a wall, by the throat. Everyone just walked past as I remember. Not even the Arsenal players chose to stop Mick in that mood.'

When asked to recall the incident, Hartford gives a wry chuckle and says, 'I don't remember that … one of many.' Hartford though won't be labelled a *hard man*. 'No, don't call me that,' he says with purpose. 'I don't like that. It's a strange definition. We were sportsman. I was brave. Call me brave. I would get in there, I wasn't afraid of getting a whack, and I got in there. I never liked the hard man tag. I would just put my head in there. That's all. I was brave.'

Of course, bravery works both ways, especially for a new centre-half arriving from distant shores and brought up on perhaps less robust strikers. Marcelino Elena had impressed with Real Mallorca in La Liga before moving to Newcastle in 1999. 'People now ask me where there was more quality in terms of forwards, England or Spain,' Elena says. 'I always said, there is a different kind of quality. In Spain it might be more technical, dribbling and so on, but in England it was about quality without the ball, about attacking crosses. Crosses were so much better in England and wingers were better at getting the ball in the box, and so the centre-forwards were the best at attacking that, and I had to adapt.

'I don't want to call it basic, because that sounds disrespectful, but there were fewer surprises with English forwards. You knew you would face longer balls, that the aerial balls had to be challenged more strongly, and then the second ball had to be won too. It was about not letting the striker take an inch.' Often easier said than done.

'My first game was at home against Aston Villa. I had played some friendlies but this was my first proper game. One big difference between the Continent and England is in the refereeing. Or it was then. In England the referee allowed a lot more contact back then. I jumped against Dion Dublin from the first goal-kick. I was used to winning 90 per cent of these challenges in Spain. Not on this occasion. Dion elbowed me, he punched me, he kicked me, we'd fall down, he'd kick me again. 'What is going on?' I would look at the ref and ask and he would look at me and shrug his shoulders as if to say, "What's wrong?" It was a big lesson.'

Elena needn't fret though – even the best have moments when such encounters can send shivers down straight spines. Alan Hansen, that doyen of central defenders, described in his autobiography, *A Matter of Opinion*, a centre-forward at Oxford who 'frightened me most'. His name was Billy Whitehurst.

Whitehurst was a well-known tyrant among the centre-half fraternity. A 6-foot Yorkshireman, weighing in at over 13 stone, Whitehurst came with a reputation akin to something out of *Grimm's Fairy Tales*; an ogre under the bridge with a taste for defensive flesh. Not surprising when, while most footballers off duty were enjoying a round of golf, Whitehurst might be found bare-knuckle fighting.

'When the fixtures were published before the season,' Hansen said, 'I would usually look at who Liverpool were playing in the first and last matches, and the dates for matches against Everton and Manchester United, our major northern rivals. When Whitehurst was at Oxford there was only one fixture I was looking for!'

Hansen's partner, Mark Lawrenson, recalls the occasion Hansen first met Whitehurst. 'I knew a bit about Billy and warned Alan. "He's mad," I warned him. Big Al took my warning with a pinch of salt, but then as he laid his eyes on him, Alan was met by a centre-forward with a load of staples in his face. He had been involved in an accident and had stitches and staples along this long scar. "Told you," I laughed.'

Another of Hansen's teammates, Steve Nicol, a footballer for all positions including centre-half, laughs at the prospect of Whitehurst – 'No one liked playing against big Billy' – but he saw up close how best to play these big players, who included Hartford and John Fashanu as well as Whitehurst.

'The thing is, they want you to be scared,' says Nicol. 'I'm not having it that big Al was really scared, whatever he said in his book. He always used to say he was nervous but he didn't seem to be. You had to use your footballing brain and if you're up against big Billy or big John Fashanu, because they want you to be scared, they want you to get in a battle with them, because it's a battle they might win. Use your brain. You don't have to challenge them. It was mostly about the big guy winning the header and flicking it on. We would try to drop off and usually the ball would fall to you from their flick. Thanks very much. It's cat and mouse. Read the second ball, don't always commit to jumping and losing the challenge because then you've left a space there.'

And what of centre-forwards playing against the more cultured centre-halves? Rosenior fancied his chances against

Hansen, but the problem was getting the ball. 'You'd go to close him down and he was gliding away. What Liverpool would do in their pomp is make the pitch massive. Wingers wide, full-backs supporting, midfield splitting, strikers on the move, centre-halves splitting, the pitch was huge so should you nick the ball, you might have a chance to exploit the space but the trouble was, you were so knackered having chased them about for a bit, that you rarely made it count. It was all about them controlling the possession and the game and that all came from their centre-backs. If you got the ball, there was a chance it would be wide open but you just didn't ever get the ball.'

Mick Hartford agrees that there were chinks of light, given the opportunity. 'Hansen and Lawrenson were the best I ever faced, but if the ball could be swung in, then you had a chance. They were great defenders, of course they were, but they weren't overly physical and they weren't aggressive so maybe the likes of me had one slight chance, but it was never easy. Their full-backs were brilliant too so crosses into the box weren't easy to come by.'

In the 1980s, Manchester United enjoyed success against Liverpool by asking their centre-forwards, Mark Hughes and Norman Whiteside or Frank Stapleton, to man mark Hansen and Lawrenson, stopping them from controlling possession. Today, the buzzword is *pressing*, but don't be fooled, it's been going on for decades. 'United got joy with that,' says Nicol. 'Especially at Old Trafford. It was a good tactic because it disturbs the way we wanted to play, but we did that to teams too. Ian Rush and Kenny Dalglish were the best at it. They would go, if I was right midfield I would be half and half, and the other team would have to go long. We often had to against United and it would become a fight in midfield, and they had the likes of Bryan

Robson and Remi Moses who could play but were more than up for a fight. I don't understand how teams can get out from defence today. It's four v four? How does that work? The forwards shouldn't be allowing it.'

So, the everlasting duel between centre-half and centre-forward has been at the very heart of the game for a century. It has been a muddy affair, and it has been a bloody affair, but even the likes of Mick Hartford – whose crooked nose alone says a thousand words about this age-old tussle – can look back with only fondness.

'I honestly believe that for all the aggression shown, there was nothing but 100 per cent respect between the players. I loved it. It's bizarre because they were all top players. Hansen, Lawrenson, Paul McGrath, Tony Adams, Dave Watson, Steve Bruce, Gary Pallister, Terry Fenwick, these guys were every bit as good as the defenders playing today, but they had to be more, they had to be physical. I made sure of that.'

Mick Hartford made sure of a lot. Dion Dublin recalls a game he played at Wimbledon while with Coventry, with his team needing a win. The Sky Blues were one up so Gordon Strachan, his manager, got Dublin back in a centre-half position he had often played, hoping to add some much-needed steel against a typical Wimbledon assault. 'I was in-between Paul Williams and Richard Shaw,' Dublin recalls. 'I would try and think like a centre-forward while playing at the back. What would they do? As the ball came in, Mick, like any good centre-forward, got himself out of my eye-line. So, I know what he is doing – as the ball is in the air, he is going to come across me from my left, with his arm up, and try and flick it on. "Concentrate, Dion," I'm telling myself, and so I jump, protect myself with a raised arm, head it as clean as you like, but his face catches my elbow flush on the right cheek and I see blood. Before my feet hit the floor, I'm concerned. This is Mick *bloody* Hartford.

'Lo and behold, the referee is calling me over. "Come 'ere, Dublin," he says. I'm walking over wondering if I'm getting sent off, but there's Mick, and I've never seen him move so fast. Blood is pissing from his face, but he's over at the ref arguing my case. "No, ref," he says, 'it was fair, that's a fair challenge, it's fine, don't send him off, leave him on." That's when I start to panic.

'I know why Mick wants me on the pitch, and it's not because he wants to swap shirts at the end. He is not going to let it lie, is he? Luckily for me, Wimbledon soon equalise and Gordon gets me back up front looking for a winner. Unfortunately for Paul Williams at the back, like me he is 6 foot 2, bald and black, and moments later he's in a heap on the floor. Mick hasn't noticed I'm no longer at centre-half, he attacks a goal-kick and it's Paul who feels his full retribution. In fact, Paul's nose is all over his face, and while he's down on the floor, Mick leans over him and says, "That'll fucking teach you, Dublin."'

And there it is, the never-ending duel between centre-half and centre-forward. But let's leave the last word to Denis Law, that most flamboyant but steely of goalscorers in the 1960s. When playing for Manchester United against Leeds, he went in for a 50-50 with his great mate, Billy Bremner, leaving more than an impression on his pal's shin. Bremner looked shell-shocked at his good friend's actions. 'Den, what are you doing?' he enquired.

'No friends on the park, son.'

Well, quite.

10

ARTISANS IN THE MUD

A Celebration of the Ball-Playing Centre-Halves

A warm New Jersey summer's evening in 1977. A well-dressed executive sits back in his leather chair, asks for more ice in his bourbon, takes a puff on his cigar, and smiles a snow-white smile, visible only through a cloud of smoke. For a moment he catches his reflection offered to him by the window of his private suite at Giants Stadium, and enjoys how god-like he looks, how divine he feels as he stares down upon the crowds who have flocked to watch his creation.

New York Cosmos are the talk of the town and beyond. An extra shot of espresso for a city that already never sleeps. Giorgio Chinaglia is the striker. Larger than life, a former giant of the Italian league. Pelé wears the number 10 shirt, the greatest, a football man who makes giants tremble.

The game kicks off, and Chinaglia and Pelé begin to make their offensive moves. Pelé might be nearing the end of his career, but his every touch and surge forward brings gasps and yelps from an admiring crowd. Each one is like the bell on a cash till to our grinning executive.

And then there's the new signing. Franz Beckenbauer. West Germany's World Cup-winning captain and sweeper. He begins to play. Organising, passing from deep, gliding across his team's back-line with all his knowing purpose.

The executive's smile begins to wane. Upturned lips droop to a grimace. Another big drag of the cigar and through the smoke, he turns quickly to a mere pawn in the corner of the room and screams, 'Tell the Kraut to get up in offence – we don't pay a million bucks for a guy to hang around in defence!'

It's a story we can all scoff at. The unknowing American money-man, his ignorance on show as much as his wealth. Money is talking, not football, and it's American money at that, and so with all our prejudices against that country and its perceived bastardisation of our game, we can sit on our high horses and laugh.

But, as we consider the centre-half and how they play, this is an interesting take on things. Centre-halves aren't there to be glamorous, are they? They aren't designed to do the pretty stuff, are they? They aren't supposed to be part of the beautiful game; in fact, to many they are the unsightly zit on its nose.

Let's consider America. In their version of football, the defence (or *dee*-fence) are stoppers, brawn not brain. The New York Cosmos executive wouldn't have seen Franz Beckenbauer, this most silky of footballers, able to move from defence into attack like brushstrokes on a canvas; he would have seen purely defence, a place that requires only courage, not skill and that, financially or aesthetically, is therefore of no interest to him.

And it's not just Americans. For many in football, the centre-half should have no part in the niceties of the game. No part in its structure or its attacking intentions. No, the centre-half, the stopper, has long been seen as prevention, not invention. Like the cork in a vintage bottle of champagne, the centre-half must keep the fizz at bay.

But what of the centre-halves who want to go pop? What of the guys who want to get the party started? The ball-playing centre-half in England has long been admired but often with reservation and even distrust. The centre-half who likes to 'get it down and play' is seen as somewhat of a luxury. A player with talent but also a player with an ego that can cause problems, problems that lose football matches.

Even Alex Ferguson, a manager who thought so much of centre-halves, building teams gluttonous for trophies, was wary of a player confusing his talent with the ball for that of another position. On signing Rio Ferdinand from Leeds for just under £30 million in 2002, the Manchester United manager was quick to give the talented, ball-playing, but sometimes strolling central defender some home truths. Ferdinand, for all his ability (and throughout the game he was known as one of the most able) there was the fear, a fear that accompanies so many centre-halves who like to 'get it down and play', that the 'get it down' bit was more important to him than the 'get it out'.

'You're a big, casual sod,' was one of the first things Ferguson said to Ferdinand when he signed him.

'I can't help it,' came the reply.

'You'll need to help it. Because it'll cost you goals, and I'll be on your back.'

It was an exchange that underlined Ferguson's desire for his defenders to defend. At Aberdeen, he had Willie Miller and Alex McLeish, at Manchester United, he had Steve Bruce and Gary Pallister, players able to play, but not ruled by a need to. In Ferdinand, he was keen on the defender, not the playmaker, but like Pallister, the ability to find a pass was an added bonus, if used in the right way.

Ferguson wasn't necessarily looking for a silky skilled, Continental type of centre-half when he signed Rio Ferdinand. It was the young Londoner's ability to read the game that counted in his favour. With his pace too, these were attributes Ferguson would later call 'non-negotiable at the top of modern football'. What he got though was a defender who would do those basics but also carry the ball from defence into attack without fuss. 'Although defending came first to me, it was encouraging to know my new centre-back could also start moves from the back, which became the norm later, with Barcelona and others,' Ferguson enthused.

The norm was a long time coming. Centre-halves in this country who liked to start things as well as stop things were rare creatures. Unicorns in football's less than enchanted forest. With the pre-war clamour for the 'stopper' centre-half, and the position losing the swashbuckling freedom it once enjoyed, a centre-half, now really only a third full-back, used his head more than his feet and the notion that he could forget about shadowing the opposing centre-forward and think creative thoughts became fanciful at best. The fun was over.

For purists though, there were green shoots of hope. Stan Cullis at Wolverhampton refused to be merely a stopper. Yes, he would embrace the challenge set by the centre-forward, he kept a book of notes, citing every centre-forward he had faced and their strengths and weaknesses, and he was no shrinking violet when it came to meeting their ire head-on, but there was more to it, there had to be. Ron Greenwood, himself a cerebral central-defender and later coach, looked up to Cullis the player, noting his all-round game and refusal to be categorised by the game's narrow approach to his position.

'Cullis combined art and conflict in the twin roles of a centre-half,' Greenwood wrote in his 1979 book, *Soccer Choice*. 'He would not accept for a moment that a centre-half should simply be an agent of destruction. He was a student of football. He had that kind of mind, always challenging and always broadcasting that knowledge. When I was at Chelsea as a player, Billy Birrell, the manager, told me to go and watch Cullis every time he came to London. "You'll never be as good as Cullis," he said. "But I want you to watch the way he plays."

'Stanley had this unmistakable crouching style, with arms and elbows working, and this made it very difficult for opponents to get near him. I remember playing against him in the war as a seventeen-year-old when he guested for Aldershot and they had a famous half-back line-up of Mercer, Cullis and Britton. They made an indelible impression on me – but Cullis most of all. There was one memorable moment when he found himself with the ball at his feet on his own goal line, just outside the penalty area and facing the crowd. One of our team, an international called Smith, a good player, moved right up behind him and there seemed no way Cullis could escape. But, still facing the crowd, his back to Smith, he started selling dummies to a man he couldn't see. His body went this way and that, the ball untouched, until he suddenly moved – the ball went with him – and Smith was left facing the crowd all by himself.'

Cullis at Wolves and then Neil Franklin at Stoke, players who wanted to do more than clear their lines. They were the minority and there were sceptics, even among those who sung their praises. Stan Mortensen, the Blackpool and England centre-forward, took both on many times. 'For many people, Cullis was a centre-half above all the others,' he said. 'He had a willingness to take a risk, holding the ball in his own penalty area and then dribbling up-field. He certainly had astute captaincy and as an outstanding player, although people will argue whether it was all for the best.'

Veiled praise and words like 'risk' and the final question of whether Cullis' thoughtful use of the ball was worth it speaks volumes of a footballing community unwilling to let the centre-half off his leash. In their 1950 book, *Soccer from the Press Box*, Archie Ledbrooke and Edgar Turner pinpointed the problem with asking centre-halves to only marshal the centre-forward and think of little else. They wrote:

> As the stopper established himself, a new problem emerged. He had solved the one of stopping the centre-forward from scoring goals, and he had perhaps gone a long way towards mastering the problem of securing the ball. But the new problem which urgently presented itself was: what was he to do with the ball? It was all very well banging it away as quickly as you drop a hot chestnut back into the hearth on a winter's evening, all very well heading the ball upfield with thick skulled energy. But the ball had a nasty habit of coming back, and you found yourself engaged in a never-ending defensive struggle which was wearying and profitless.

Ledbrooke and Turner were underlining the need for thought. Agricultural defending would be hard to shift but in the likes of Cullis, there was another way, a better way. 'Cullis had courage,' they wrote. 'He was not afraid to stop the ball in the heart of the game in his own penalty area, and he never hesitated to attempt to beat a man to give himself more room for his clearance kick … Able to trick a man, Cullis could make a little ground and deliver a short pass to a wing-half or an inside-forward, and it was this perfection of football which made him such an outstanding figure in the years immediately before the second war.'

Another figure impressed by Cullis was a young Dennis Wilshaw, who played alongside the centre-half as a teenager during the war and would go on to play under Cullis when he became manager at Wolves. 'He was a brilliant ball player,' Wilshaw noted. 'What mystified me was the way he used to pull the ball down in a defensive position and do a little shimmy-shammy with it. When he was a manager he would never let us do anything like that.'

That's the thing. A player might have the courage to play, the courage to take a risk, drop a shoulder, but those picking the team and coaching the team, those whose job is on the line if risks are taken, they might see things differently, however brazenly they played the game.

The most forward-thinking manager and coach of recent times has been Pep Guardiola. It is said that Guardiola would like a team of midfielders, players able to play. He has no qualms moving midfielders to centre-half. Javier Mascherano, to look at him, was not a centre-half, but he was more than successful there for Guardiola's Barcelona, able to spoil and then play.

When Guardiola came to Manchester City and spent a lot of money on England's John Stones, the coach was questioned by the press about the young defender's worrying habit of making mistakes, mistakes that led to chances, chances that led to goals. 'John Stones has more personality than all of us here in this room,' the coach told the press conference. 'More balls than everyone here. I like that. I love him. Under pressure, the people criticise him, so I am delighted to have John. With all his huge amount of mistakes. I love him. I love guys with this personality. Because it's not easy to play central defender with this manager. It's not easy. You have to defend 40 metres behind and make the build-up.'

Guardiola demands courage to match his own, but even the greatest managers down the years have scoffed at a central defender showing what they saw merely as delusions of grandeur. 'Cloughie fined me once for playing a square pass,' ex-Nottingham Forest defender Kenny Burns says of Brian Clough.

'Shilts rolled it to me, and he wanted it back. I thought, "Fuck you." I chipped it across the eighteen-yard box to Colin Barrett. We were playing Manchester City and Denis Tueart got a touch on it, pushing it out for a goal-kick. I put my hand up and said, "Sorry, my fault," and got on with things. Cloughie though wasn't having it and at half-time, I think we were three up or something but he laid into me. "At the end of the day, this is your career, you have to learn," he said. He fined me 50 quid, half my wages for that square pass. Bloody hell! I learnt that if you don't need to take chances, then there is no need. Take it easy. It was a good lesson. I had too many great players around me who could get a simple pass from me. No need to mess about. The only time a centre-half should dribble is when he's drunk!'

Now Brian Clough was far from a pragmatic manager keen on merely booting the ball to safety. It was he after all who said, 'If God had wanted us to play football in the clouds, he would've put grass up there.' But in a results business, even the most flamboyant of football thinkers, when it comes to centre-halves with ambitions of playmaking, will lose their nerve.

George Graham was the most flamboyant of footballers. In the 1960s and 1970s with Chelsea, Arsenal and then Manchester United, the Scottish midfielder earned the nickname 'Stroller' for his nonchalant style of play. All sideburns and swagger. On signing for Chelsea in 1964, dressed in a shimmering new three-piece suit, new teammate John Collins thought he was a model walking in off the Kings Road.

Later though, with the tailored suit swapped for the track version, things changed. Being at Arsenal had instilled hitherto untapped discipline in Graham and his football teams would mirror his new outlook. Players might moan. The Swede Anders Limpar said that working with him was like, 'Living with Saddam Hussein in Iraq'. The club's creative players would raise an eyebrow at how much Graham worked with his back four, having them all moving as one holding a rope. Graham's former teammate and great friend Frank McLintock said, 'George Graham, the manager, would never have picked George Graham, the footballer, for his team.'

'It's true, I wouldn't,' Graham agreed, and the effect his methods had on the club's back four and goals against column says it all. Tony Adams, Steve Bould, Martin Keown: talented centre-halves, but under Graham they were discouraged to be pretty on the ball. They were a unit, not individuals. 'I used to say that I planted my bulbs in the garden in a strong defensive line,' Graham liked to quip.

Pushing for honours in the late 1980s and early 1990s meant taking on Liverpool, a team who had excelled at home and abroad using centre-halves who, while scolded to defend,

THOU SHALL NOT PASS

were encouraged to play. Alan Hansen and Mark Lawrenson had become bywords for defensive creativity, and Gary Gillespie had seamlessly replaced the latter. More of them later, but for some younger centre-halves at the time, envious eyes were cast towards Anfield.

'It really used to get on my nerves when Hansen and Lawrenson were passing the ball about and getting all this praise,' Tony Adams would write in his autobiography, *Addicted*. 'I knew I was capable of all that. Sometimes I thought they should just have kicked the ball clear, like I did and was instructed to. Later, I reckoned I would come to pass the ball as well as they ever did.'

Adams' shackles came off playing under Terry Venables with England and then Arsène Wenger at Arsenal. These were managers and coaches with different approaches to a central defender's duties, but these are individuals. What of clubs who, dictated to by their past and with it ingrained in their DNA, demand that their centre-halves play? West Ham United can profess to be such a club.

Bobby Moore in the number 6 shirt, blond locks, untarnished shorts despite his muddy arena; a symbol of central defensive grace that will last long into the club's and the country's future. Moore was the product of a philosophy. Under Ted Fenton, West Ham had, in 1957/58, not only won their first promotion to the top flight since 1932, but established 'The Academy', a seat of learning where a blueprint could be passed down through the generations.

Fenton encouraged his players to take their coaching badges and in Malcolm Allison, his big, commanding but skilful centre-half, he had a diligent pupil, eager to cajole from a young player, a particular way of playing his position. That young player was Bobby Moore. Not many saw much in Moore, this slightly chubby, slow boy from Essex. Allison though saw everything and demanded the club give the boy their last place in the youth set-up. 'I was the thirteenth player on the ground staff,' Moore later said. 'I was ordinary. I was lucky to be there. And every time I looked at the other lads, I knew it … All around me were players with unbelievable ability. They were the same age as me and I was looking up to them and wishing I was that good, that skilful.'

With Allison at his back and in his ear, soon he would be and English football would have a new beacon of hope. 'Bobby used to swear to me that he would not have made it as a footballer without Malcolm Allison,' says Harry Redknapp, a one-time teammate of Moore's at West Ham. 'Malcolm used to train the kids. Senior pros would do that on a Tuesday and Thursday to earn a few more quid. Malcolm was into coaching and he'd happily take the thirteen- or fourteen-year-olds. Malcolm coached young Bobby and he loved him. No one else could see anything in Bobby, but Malcolm did.

'He'd drive Bobby home back to Barking and chat to him about the game. When Bobby left school there was only one place left on the ground staff. Everyone at the club wanted to give it to this other kid, but Malcolm thought they were mad. The staff were adamant but Malcolm – who was pretty much the boss of West Ham as a player – stepped in and said, "No, you're taking Bobby. This kid will be a player." They argued that Bobby couldn't run, but Malcolm said, "No, this kid will be some player," and they listened.'

Also having to listen was the young Moore, and after one game against the Chelsea youth team, the youngster was made to realise that he should, and he would, play the game in a certain way. 'Barry Bridges was playing for Chelsea,' recalls Redknapp. 'Barry had played for Chelsea's first team and scored on the Saturday but was put back in the youth team on the Tuesday. Managers wouldn't want youngsters to get big for their boots, so you were back in the youth team with your mates.

'Barry never got a sniff. Bobby marked him out the game. Bobby stuck to him the whole game. In the dressing room he was feeling well pleased with himself. Malcolm walked in and rather than saying, "Well done," he said, "If I ever see you play like that again, I'll never talk to you again."

'Malcolm's point was, Bobby – when the keeper got the ball – was running forward and marking Barry. That wouldn't do. Malcolm was furious that when the full-back had it, Bobby wasn't giving him an angle, wasn't dropping in to take the pass, he wasn't getting it off the keeper, starting things, playing. That wouldn't do and Malcolm told him. Well, Bobby went on and did just that, didn't he? He'd come deep, get it, give to the full-back, get it back and bang, a perfect pass into Hursty's [Geoff Hurst's] feet. Bullseye.'

And with that the tone was set. Centre-halves in West Ham's claret and blue were expected to play a certain way. Many would, and with perhaps no great shame, fall short, but managers such as Sam Allardyce trying to play a certain, and perhaps necessary way, would hear disapproval from a set of fans used to or brought up on tales of that bullseye. Billy Bonds, Rio Ferdinand, today perhaps Declan Rice, all carry Moore's (and Allison's) mantle. One such player was Tony Gale.

Gale started at Fulham, where he was apprentice to Bobby Moore. 'That was an education,' Gale says. 'I learnt so much from him, how not to waste a pass. I had the philosophy that my position was not only about defending but also the first line of attack.

'I followed Bobby into the Fulham first team, and then moved to West Ham. I took so much from his technique with the ball. I'd watch him play off the front foot, rather than the back foot. By that I mean he could get the ball out of his feet quicker and play with maybe the outside of the foot, because the quicker you could release it, the quicker you were on the attack. Strikers would love it if you played it earlier.

'West Ham, like Fulham, was great for me, because at Upton Park, ball-playing centre-backs were a necessity. John Lyall expected me to start attacks. A lot of clubs actively discouraged their centre-backs to play. The great Arsenal back four were told not to play it out under George Graham. "Don't take a risk," was the norm.

'I would look to get it and get it to a forward. Bobby used to say, "Can you get it to the feet of a striker?" I would also use the midfield area as a set-up pass. Get it in to one of them but want it back and then there will be space for a ball into the strikers or in down the sides of the centre-back, where they hate it. I'd hate it when a midfield would come close to me and look to get it right off my toes. "What are you doing? Piss off. I can carry the ball. You give me an angle and let's go.'"

What West Ham wanted, what they want, is players first, players who can defend sure, but the likes of Moore, Bonds, Ferdinand, they learnt to play in midfield before stepping back. It was a belief that Liverpool would build their dominance of the Continental game upon. Bill Shankly had used his 'colossus', Ron Yeats, at centre-half in his early WM formation, but would often put Tommy Smith back there with him in early dalliances with a back four.

After humbling defeats to Ajax and then Red Star Belgrade in the European Cup, Shankly and his canny staff realised that glory in the European game especially required a more subtle approach. Championships had been won with the dominant Larry Lloyd (Lloyd would later do great things at home and in Europe with Brian Clough's Nottingham Forest) but Liverpool would opt for a less robust approach.

Emlyn Hughes and Phil Thompson were paired at the back; both were good on the ball, both midfielders at heart. 'He drummed into us to play from the back,' says Phil Thompson. 'Larry Lloyd had got injured and Shanks threw me, a defensive midfielder, in at centre-back alongside another midfielder, Emlyn Hughes. You normally had a commanding centre-back with a ball player next to him, but now Shanks had two ball players.

'That was the clue to the type of football that Shanks had us playing. It was so patient. We'd play a high line but Clem [Ray Clemence] would sweep behind us, get the ball, give it to us, we'd feed the full-backs and it would go from there.'

Shankly's successors would follow suit, with Alan Hansen replacing Hughes and then Mark Lawrenson replacing Thompson. Trophies followed trophies. What these ball-playing centre-halves lacked in the big, physical, even brutish side of the game, they made up for with forward-thinking nobility. Hansen and Lawrenson both enjoyed stints in midfield early in their careers, giving them (like those before them) not only an enjoyment for the feel of the ball at their feet, but the desire to win the ball in a way that kept possession.

In the early spring of 1988, at his pomp, Alan Hansen faced an eager young Nottingham Forest team at Anfield. The ball is played gingerly forward from Forest's midfield to young Lee Glover, but rather than making a firm tackle from behind on the striker (as was his right back then), Hansen steps in on the player's left-hand side, and, using his right foot, glides forward with the ball before calmly playing a ten-yard pass and setting up the opening goal. John Motson from the commentary box said, 'Experience against innocence, there perhaps.' Motson was right, but it was also defensive guile against defensive boorishness. It was a trait that other talented centre-halves shared. By winning the ball rather than merely tackling the player, a centre-half with their momentum moving them forward becomes an extra player in attack. Opposing defenders are on the back foot and panic ensues.

'It's such a skill,' says Tony Gale. 'Bobby Moore had it too, and I liked to intercept rather than go through people. Some defenders liked to go through the striker, get their boots down the back of his Achilles or calves, but I wanted to intercept and then keep the ball. Today it's called transition and celebrated. When I played, the crowd preferred the big tackle. Ball in Row Z and the forward in a heap on the floor.'

Gary Pallister at Manchester United enjoyed a dynasty-forming partnership with Steve Bruce but much of their compatibility came from their different approaches to their art. Andrew Cole, who played against them before playing with them, saw it first-hand. 'Steve was a brilliant footballer,' he says. 'Strong, clever, he might have lacked pace but no one ever ran him, because he was on top of you. Pally was his opposite. Whereas Bruce would come through you and beat you with force, Pally would try to nick the ball away from you, stretch in front of you and steal possession from you.' With that approach, possession – that most bullion-like commodity in the game – can be kept and treasured.

That's what Hansen brought to Liverpool. Pallister to United. Gale, like Bobby Moore before him, to West Ham. The treasure of possession. Mark Lawrenson, long-term partner of Hansen and himself a devout keeper of the ball, had a ringside seat for his teammate's ability. 'Bobby Robson brought an England team to Anfield for a testimonial and Micky Channon was playing,' recalls Lawrenson. 'Someone put a ball down the channel on Alan's side and Micky had yards on him. Al just glided across, took it off him, knocked it and passed it. "Fuckin' 'ell," Micky shouted in that West Country accent. "He's not fuckin' real."

'The thing about Al was that the game was too easy for him. We'd play on the worst pitches and Al would come off, having played the best game with his kit clean. He could take it off, give it to the kit man and tell him not to bother washing it. You never, ever panicked him. The times he made a mistake or gave the ball away were minimal. Don't tell him I said all that though!'

It would be wrong though to think that Liverpool's tactics were relaxed. Simply pass the ball nicely out of defence? No chance. '"Stay in your armchairs!" That's what Ronnie Moran would shout at Al and me,' says Lawrenson. 'If we were under pressure, the shout was, "Stay in your armchairs!" By that he meant for us not to go anywhere, nothing flash. Keep the shape and don't get caught out of position. When we heard that, it was clear, keep it simple.'

Lawrenson found out early in his career at Anfield that being clever on the ball at centre-half, while expected to an extent, could run a fine line with cockiness. 'One Saturday, I dropped the shoulder a couple of times at Highbury, sold Tony Woodcock and carried the ball away. Jimmy Hill highlighted it on *Match of the Day* that night, and on the Monday, Bob [Paisley] passed me at training.

'"What did you do on Saturday night?" he asked.

'"Nothing, boss."

'"Did you watch *Match of the Day*?"

'"Yes, I did".

'"Well, so did everybody else."

'By that he meant every player saw that trick and they will be ready next time. Took me down a peg or two but I got it.'

Paisley's gentle nod towards conservatism was one thing, but managers such as him and today Pep Guardiola and Jürgen Klopp do ask their centre-halves to have courage. Big balls even. But courage isn't just putting your head in where it hurts. Harry Redknapp, teammate of Bobby Moore, noted that like Hansen, his kit kept its sheen, but never doubted that Moore was the bravest of players.

'Oh yeah,' says Redknapp. 'Bobby was great at that. He could read the game and read danger. The country love how stylish a footballer Bobby was, but he would do the rough stuff. He lacked pace but he didn't need it. He could be on a striker because he read the danger and he loved a late block. Never seemed to get that muddy somehow but no, he was as brave as he was good.'

Bravery comes in different forms. Waiting to make your tackle. Staying on your feet until the perfect moment. Moore's tackle on Jairzinho in the 1970 World Cup remains as brave a defensive moment as it is iconic. 'What he would do was when people ran him, he would bide his time,' says Redknapp.

'Jairzinho has ripped everyone to bits in Mexico, but not Bobby. That tackle is great but the whole game, Bobby waited and ran him to the corner or timed a perfect tackle. He did that to me every day in training. Fantastic.'

Today, the modern centre-half who wants to play is still met with a degree of scepticism. An English centre-half getting the ball, looking for a pass, looking to get that pass back, get things moving forward is smiled at, politely applauded, but too often thoughts rush to a worst-case scenario. 'He's a mistake waiting to happen,' comes the murmur.

Virgil van Dijk isn't having it though, embracing just how vital the position is and how vital a centre-half is when it comes to getting on the ball. 'It's more important today, the position. A lot more. Nowadays playing out from the back is a huge thing, especially for teams who like to be in possession of the ball. The bigger teams in world football want to have players who are comfortable on the ball, even in their own box and around it. Being under pressure, players who get on the ball can be a massive help.

'Back in the day, maybe centre-halves were expected to not get involved. Give the ball to the midfielders and then your task is to simply make sure the defensive organisation is there and to defend the goal. Now everyone is getting involved. You still have to do those duties, but there is so much more asked of defenders and the position has developed. The full-back position is changing too, they are almost like wingers in our Liverpool team but they must also do their defending too. The game has developed. I enjoy every bit of it. I am a player who likes to have the ball and hopefully I make good decisions that help the team, not only defensively but offensively too.

'We have Alisson, who is not afraid to pick a pass. We all have to be confident in our own ability to make it happen. The most important thing is that you do it when you think you can do it, not to be clever for the sake of it. If I am feeling under pressure and I sense danger, I can tell Alisson to kick the ball up front and we will play for the second ball. We have that diversity, we can mix it up, playing it short and playing it long. That is important and one of our real strengths.

'We can adapt. At the end of the day, you are responsible. If I want the ball, and I make the mistake, it is my fault. I don't want to put myself in that situation if I sense it isn't going to go right. Why do it? To look good? No way!'

Steph Houghton agrees that the fashion for ball-playing central defenders is far from showboating, and instead is the catalyst for her club's tactical approach. 'I love having the ball at my feet. I like to be able to control the game, and I think we can these days. At City, we concentrate on playing out from the back, and even when we face a heavy press, you have to be brave. I like it. It's high risk, but I like it. Our keeper and the other centre-halves and the midfield, we all relish it. We get a high press but we work on patterns of play and yes, we relish the challenge, because if we beat that press then the team can be away. It's about manipulating the forwards, overloading in certain areas, inviting the press and then we are away. The technical ability has to be there. It starts from the back and a lot of our goals come from that.'

Joe Worrall is a young centre-half at Nottingham Forest, and captained the England under-21s to victory at the 2017 Toulon Tournament. He looks at his position still with a degree of conservatism. 'Every manager I have had has advised me not to get too caught up in passing out from the back,' he says. 'Of course they want me to be tidy and do the right things but my job is to keep the ball out of the net. Football in the Championship is different of course, I get that, but we are very geared towards keeping clean sheets first and maybe playing second. That might change one day when I am playing in the Premier League, but for now, still learning the game, I am more keen on the defensive side of things.

'I do look at how many times I have touched the ball. Not so much success rate, more how many times I have got involved. If it comes to me on the halfway line and someone is pressing me, I will happily just head it back into the mix or whatever. I manage risk. I will look before I receive it to know if I can take one, two, or even three touches. I don't want to have three touches though, I just want to get it and give it.'

John Stones, Guardiola's defender with the big balls, a player who likes to get it and give it and get it some more, has come in for scrutiny. His desire to play is used as an excuse to scrutinise the spit-and-sawdust side of his game. In his autobiography, *Sober*, Tony Adams picked out the England centre-half when arguing that the nation has a habit of overpraising young talent. 'For example, John Stones was hailed as a great new English central defender, first at Everton and then at Manchester City,' Adams wrote. 'I have always had my doubts about him, considered him to be average in all honesty, despite this hyping of him as a ball-using defender. I saw him as a Tony Gale, a centre-half who passed the ball well, and was good enough to win a Premier League title with Blackburn Rovers, but who did not win an England cap. Such is the dearth of English ball-playing defenders, though, that Manchester City were willing to pay £50 million for Stones.'

Guardiola might argue otherwise, and Tony Gale certainly would. 'I would never change my style,' he says. 'I read what Tony said about me in his book and that is fine. Tony wasn't a great passer of the ball. He was more of a leader. His passing improved but his game was all about his commitment to the cause. I'd always like to be remembered as a footballer.'

Today, centre-halves at the top of the game must be footballers. The pitches are perfect, the rules would rather they passed than tackled and the coaches encourage their art. Will the public ever embrace them as artisans, though? After the 2019 Ballon d'Or was announced, the journalist Henry Winter wrote a column for *The Times* underlining why he voted for Liverpool's centre-half Virgil van Dijk rather than Barcelona maestro Lionel Messi. The headline ran, 'I Resisted Clamour for Glamour and Voted van Dijk'. That's the thing; that's *still* the thing. Centre-halves aren't suited to glamour. To many they are more red cards than red carpets. That old 1977 New York Cosmos executive would raise his bourbon to that.

11

DEADLY DUOS

The Great Partnerships

William Shakespeare liked partnerships. He enjoyed the tragedy, the romance and the comedy that spins from them. What then would the Bard have made of centre-half pairings? The centre of defence, that spot on a football pitch where tragedy, romance and a lot of comedy are regular by-products. There's Sol Campbell and Tony Adams, Arsenal's double-winning pairing of 2002, a *Romeo and Juliet* of sorts – forbidden partners, one stepping out from the enemy to be with the other. Or John Terry and Marcel Desailly at Chelsea – Stamford Bridge's *Antony and Cleopatra*, two giants from two different empires. Then there is Malcolm Shotton and Gary Briggs at Oxford United in the 1980s – actually just two *Richard IIIs*, both with the hump.

Much has been made of partnerships in football, mostly though those of the attacking kind. People sit and people ponder; what makes two strikers hit it off? Theatrical musings worthy of those who tread Shakespearean boards are used; terms such as *chemistry* and *telepathy* roll from the tongue. 'The big man playing off the little man' … 'one style complementing the other' … 'they are the complete package'. All very nice, but less eulogising has gone on about central defensive pair ups. Stick two bigguns back there to look after things, that'll do it.

And sometimes it does, but as the modern game has evolved, as possession based football has became *de rigueur*, a centre-half pairing became as important and as nuanced as any on the pitch. Reasons could be simple ('Bobby wasn't that great in the air so England stuck Jack Charlton next to him' – Harry Redknapp) or they could be slightly deeper ('I've always said you see into your teammate's soul when you play with them for a while' – Terry Butcher), but what has become clear is duos at the back and how they gel is vital.

Centre-half partnerships became the norm in Britain in the early to mid-1960s when the usual WM formation, pretty much universally used since the late 1920s, started to be broken up and a 4-4-2, 4-2-4 or 4-3-3 became the norm, giving us football analogists a more rigid spine, and our two vertebrae at the back were introduced to each other on a regular basis.

As early as 1962, Jack Charlton at Leeds was in and out of the side, and often used at centre-forward. He went to his manager, Don Revie, with some stern words. Revie had Freddie Goodwin, his usual centre-half, playing a man-marking system at the back. It wasn't working. Relegation to the Third Division had been narrowly avoided but with the promise that he would be the regular marshal in defence, Charlton had some ideas.

'There was a game against Swansea, in September 1962, that marked a turning point in my life,' Charlton later said. 'Don had left a lot of the senior players out of the side, a very brave thing to do at the time, and he brought in a lot of new young players he'd just signed – Gary Sprake in goal, Norman Hunter, Paul Reaney, and a fellow called Rod Johnson. I said to Don, "Well, I'm not going to play the way you've been playing with Fred. I don't want to play man-to-man marking, I want to play a zonal system where you pick up people in your area. I'll sort out the back four for you the way I want them to play" – and Don said OK.

'That, for me, was the moment when I stopped being one of the awkward squad and came on board the Leeds United ship. It was a sign that I would be one of the key players in the new team Don was building. I was sort of the organiser at the back, I was the pusher, I was the one who told the young lads where to go, when to cover, and how to pick up positions.' An infamous and successful partnership was born. Charlton and Hunter would be synonymous with 1960s dynamism, the scourge of many forward lines, but in time the young Hunter learnt from the master and orders became harder to take.

'I'll never forget something that happened a few years later,' Charlton continued. 'Norman Hunter suddenly rebelled against me telling him what to do. "I've been with you long enough and I've learned my bloody lesson now," he said. "I wish you'd let me do things my way instead of you bloody telling me all the time."

'And I said, "Norman, now you're reacting that way, you're fine. Get on with it."

'He reminded me of me.'

Good communication, you see, but also there must be an acknowledgement of each other's differences. When Bobby Moore received the ball on the edge of his box in the final moments of the 1966 World Cup final, and with eager German forwards falling in around him, his partner Jack Charlton could be heard screaming at him to punt the ball over the twin towers and on to the Metropolitan Line tube tracks. Instead, Moore dribbled, weaved and got Geoff Hurst on his way to a hat-trick.

Moore would look back with affection for his World Cup winning partner, a man and a footballer cut from a different cloth to his own. 'Jack Charlton?' he said. 'A big man and a big character. Some days we'd be going out and I'd look at him and wonder how the hell this giraffe played football. But he was tremendously effective. We used to argue black and blue because I wanted to get the ball down and play the game and he wanted to hoof it away to safety. But we made a pair.'

Centre-half partnerships would often celebrate such contrasts. At club level, Charlton played alongside Hunter, who like Moore enjoyed the feel of the ball on his leathery toes. At Manchester City in the early 1970s, the hard Mancunian Mike Doyle, a good footballer but as the son of a policeman and trained in unarmed combat never shirked the physical; dovetailed astutely with his teammate Tony Booth, a player the former Manchester City manager Joe Mercer called 'the best footballing centre-half since Stan Cullis'. It was a late 1960s and early 1970s partnership that won FA Cup and League Cup medals.

Paul Elliott finished his career at Chelsea and is an advocate of centre-halves celebrating their differences and understanding the other's methods. Two big personalities might just hinder all that. 'In the UK they played traditionally a No. 5 as a stopper, the enforcer and the No. 6 as the more footballing type,' says Elliott. 'It was important their characteristics were complimentary. In generations of the old First Division the centre-halves played as a pair. That's very much the same today. When I was at Chelsea in 1991 the same partnership principles were applicable. I played alongside a young, emerging Jason Cundy. He listened well, took instructions and we forged a good understanding. It was different with Ken Monkou, who was a colossus of a defender, a physical specimen to be revered. He was, though, very unpredictable, very talented and dominant, but we never consistently aligned as a complimentary pair, which at times presented challenges. We would compete for the same ball rather than one attack and one cover behind.'

History shows that great success can be had by playing two centre-halves who were seemingly chalk and cheese. Brian Clough's Nottingham Forest would dominate the fields of England and Europe at the end of the decade, housing the giant stopper, Larry Lloyd, and the perhaps more deft, one-time centre-forward, Kenny Burns. A big man, smaller man pairing. But only on the face of it.

'When I signed for Forest, I wasn't sure where Cloughie wanted to play me,' Burns recalls. 'We went to Germany for pre-season, and we played first team against the second team. Cloughie was away on holiday, God knows where, but Peter Taylor was there and the teams were read out. I was in with the first team, with Larry Lloyd, and so I thought, I'm the centre-back here. Fine by me. No problems.

'We were very different to look at, Larry and me, but we weren't asked to play some sort of system off of each other. Larry was like a runaway car anyway, and loved to attack things, but so did I. It was quite simple. Larry and I understood each other. Our full-backs too. Viv [Anderson] was to my left, Colin [Barrett] was to Larry's right and we all knew each other's games, helping each other. In that sense the team was like a car, and we were like spark plugs. If one of us went, the car couldn't start.

'Larry and I worked on things, you have to, but I worked with Viv too. With Larry, it was right and left. I go or he goes. Very simple. If we have a corner against us, Viv and Colin on posts, John McGovern at the front, I am in the middle, and Larry on the back. Kind of zonal but more about taking responsibility. That simple. We didn't really man mark.'

There are plenty of those who have worked in the modern game who remain fans of contrasting styles at the back. See it as the ideal. 'Yeah, I like to see a bit of difference,' says Harry Redknapp. 'When I was managing, I looked to have a biggun, a player who liked to attack things in the air, but alongside him someone a bit more comfortable on the ball, someone who can play a bit.'

That's the thing, contrasts worked. To look at Terry Butcher and his partner Russell Osman at Ipswich Town during the Suffolk club's halcyon period saddling the 1970s and 1980s, the two men were opposites. Butcher, perfectly named, meaty, rare, imposing, a centre-half's centre-half. Osman, with his matinee idol looks and calm authority. Both had learnt from Allan Hunter and Kevin Beattie at Portman Road before going on to make the loss of those two legends far from a problem.

'You work at it and we did,' says Butcher. 'We had a nice balance. Right- and left-footed. You have to play with the man a few times, you get used to their movements, their strengths, and weaknesses. It's all about understanding. I always said you see into your teammate's soul when you play with them for a while. You see what sort of person he is. If he is a bit lazy then you know when to get him going. You talk to them so much and you work that out between you. The position needs communication more than any other. We're lucky as the game is all ahead of us.'

Russell Osman (the centre-half whose soul Butcher most effectively looked into) agrees and even mirrors his former partner's sentiments. 'The "special" part of our relationship was probably a bit of a telepathic understanding of how we saw the game situations developing in front of us and how we dealt with them,' Osman says.

'I think we just seemed to complement each other in the way that we played. Terry knew that I would compete against anybody in the air and I was confident in Terry's ability, both on the ball and in one-on-one situations. But please make no mistake about the fact that we both had to work very hard on a daily basis to improve both our weaknesses and strengths, being physically competitive was part and parcel of training, you cannot just switch it on for a match-day, plus we had some very tough coaches to please.

'Off the pitch, we had some fantastic nights together – well, some were day/night/mornings, a few curfews were broken along the way, but would get a rollicking from the management and move on professionally until the next curfew got broken. We had a team that worked hard and played hard, we were fitter than most teams and you knew if you came in feeling the worse for wear after a late night then you would be expected to put in an extra bit of effort in the morning to get it out of your system.

'When we were both "on our game" there were very few strike partnerships that would give us too many problems, if we were having a bad day then they all gave us problems. Dalglish and Rush were always a handful, but we had some very good results against Liverpool in those days. We were also very fortunate to be playing in a very good team.

'Robson encouraged me to not get so involved in the games and to try and read the games more, be more thoughtful rather than more physical. He told me to play like Bobby Moore, always be in the right place at the right time, and when in possession of the ball, play the way that Ipswich play, by passing the ball to each other. If you could play an early long pass to a striker then that was always the best option, if not keep the ball by playing it through the midfield.'

John Clark and Billy McNeill in Jock Stein's conquering Celtic side were very different. McNeill was dominant and combative, Clark deeper, willing to drop and sweep. 'I had quite a good reputation for reading the game,' Clark says. 'They called me "The Brush" as I would work behind my other defenders and with big Billy, it was a good combination. Not many players in Europe were as good in the air as Billy, so sometimes I was left with little to do! Billy would go and challenge the big aerial balls, and he was facing the biggest and best players in Europe, but we could play too. We were getting the ball off the keeper all the time, that's how Jock wanted us to play, and the two of us enjoyed that. It came naturally to us. We didn't work hard on it on the training ground. We had a natural chemistry, I suppose.'

At Manchester United, Paul McGrath and Kevin Moran offered silk and steel, and their eventual replacements in Alex Ferguson's team, Steve Bruce and Gary Pallister – or Dolly and Daisy, as their manager affectionately named them – while both fantastic defenders, they went about their business slightly differently, with Pallister less bombastic (compare their noses for proof) than his Geordie partner. Playing 800 games for the club between them, strikers in the 1990s were regularly consumed by their dual brilliance, and they could even aid the side offensively, most notably in 1993, when, into injury time and drawing 1–1 at Old Trafford against Sheffield Wednesday and with an elusive title on the line, Pallister found himself on the right wing, and like a prophetic incarnation of a yet-to-be-discovered David

Beckham, he swung a right-footed cross in, which Bruce met with his substantial forehead to send the ball into the net and the Stretford End into raptures.

There are other subtle examples. John Terry and the Portuguese Ricardo Carvalho complemented each other perfectly at the heart of Chelsea's resurgence in the 2000s. Carvalho, after a slow start coping with the perpetual motion of the English game, was perfect for Terry. Yes, Terry was a stopper of sorts but he was a wonderful reader of the ball's thoughts, able to be where it would be with sheer perception and determination. However, if things got pacy, Carvalho was on hand to combat it with rockets in his boots. Two different players, from different places, brought together as a wall in José Mourinho's brilliant first team.

'In my first year here, it was hard for me because I was at a new club, in a new country, in a new league and playing a much more physical kind of game than I was used to in Portugal,' Carvalho would say. 'JT recognised this straight away and was such a big help, on and off the pitch. He really made me feel comfortable. He is one of the best I've played with and a great leader too. He is stronger than me and likes to get in the air whereas I play more with the ball than him. But that is what makes us such a good partnership together. As a centre-half, whoever you are playing with, you have to know your partner very well and have an understanding. It's like being two halves of the same whole. Instinctively, I have to know what he is going to do and he has to know what I'm going to do. The understanding between the two players is very important.'

Chelsea's dominance in the middle of the decade was followed by Manchester United's at its end, and like Chelsea, in Nemanja Vidić and Rio Ferdinand the side had two players, one (Vidić) more aggressive while Ferdinand was born to carry the ball forward. Both though could carry out the other man's strengths and both were hell-bent on clean sheets. The twenty-eight they helped keep in the 2008/09 season is testimony to their stubbornness.

The partnership at Liverpool of Virgil van Dijk and Joe Gomez again celebrates different styles. Van Dijk is two inches taller (and six years older) than his partner, and at first liked to dominate the aerial stuff, but such is the progression of the younger man, he attacks the ball with all the confidence of the Dutchman, and they are able to dovetail perfectly at the heart of Liverpool's defence. 'Van Dijk and Gomez have the attributes to deal with anyone,' says Martin Keown, no stranger himself to decent partnerships. 'Up against the best sides, you want Rolls-Royces at centre-back and rarely can I remember a partnership that boasts so much pace. I was two inches shorter than Tony Adams but backed myself to win every header that came my way.'

But are differences, however subtle, the only way? In the early 1970s, teams chasing success at home and abroad looked for a change from the notion of two styles complementing the other. At Derby, under Brian Clough, the side relied on Roy McFarland and Colin Todd, two players cut from the same marbleised granite. Both able to compete in the ever-so-competitive top flight, while both hungry to get on the ball and get Clough's team moving.

Todd had been well-schooled in the art of central defending at Sunderland by the great Charlie Hurley, a classy defender from the Irish Republic and voted the club's, 'Player of the Century' by the fans to mark the club's centenary in 1979. Together they formed a still-talked-of partnership at Roker Park, before Clough swooped to take the younger man (one he had known from his days working with the Sunderland youth team) to Derby's Baseball Ground. There, Todd alongside McFarland would make a mockery of the old ground's notoriously mud-quenched turf, moving the ball around as if playing on satin. In 1972 and 1975, the First Division titles were won and in 1973, the side were desperately unlucky to lose to Juventus in the semi-final of the European Cup.

Ah yes, European glory and the quest for it. In 1973, Bill Shankly's Liverpool won the championship in style, their centre-half pairing Larry Lloyd and Tommy Smith, players that put the rock in bedrock. Another crack at the European Cup, that trophy already won by Shankly's friends and Scottish south lowland comrades, Jock Stein and Matt Busby. But Liverpool were beaten 4–2 on aggregate by Red Star Belgrade, and the strange ease the Yugoslavs won in each leg was enough to make Shankly and his boot-room staff rethink matters. However good Liverpool's dynamic, fast game was under Shankly, a new approach was needed in a changing game.

'The Europeans showed that building from the back is the only way to play,' Shankly explained after his retirement. 'It started in Europe and we adapted it into our game at Liverpool, where our system had always been a collective one. But when Phil Thompson came in to partner [Emlyn] Hughes, it became more fluid and perhaps not as easy to identify. This set the pattern which was followed by Thompson and [Alan] Hansen in later years.'

And so it began. Liverpool's success, already budding in the 1960s and early 1970s, would now grow forest-like, with a game based on possession and a team based on two strong, yes, but ball-playing centre-halves. Mark Lawrenson would replace Thompson, Gary Gillespie would replace Lawrenson, and Glenn Hysén would replace Gillespie. Now with their first title won since those heady days, the central defence partnership has gone back to brilliant basics.

From goalkeeper to centre-half and to full-back, into the midfield, back to centre-half and so on. Patient. 'We realised at Liverpool that you can't score a goal every time you get the ball. And we learned this from the Europeans, from the Latin people,' Shankly said. 'When they play from the back they play in little groups. The pattern of the opposition changes as they change. This leaves room for players like Ray Kennedy and Terry McDermott, who both played for Liverpool after I left, to sneak in for the final pass. So it's cat and mouse for a while, waiting for the opening to appear before the final ball is let loose. It's simple and it's effective.'

Or *efficax* if we're talking *effective* in Latin, and for two of Liverpool's (and English football's) most hallowed centre-halves, that's a language – as well as being fluent in defending – they both understood. 'Yes, both me and Al got our Latin O-levels,' laughs Mark Lawrenson. 'We got on very well from the moment we met. Eventually that showed in how we played as we had so much trust in each other. We were semi-intelligent, big mates off the pitch, but never really had to speak much on it. That's a trust thing and an understanding. Thinking about it, I don't think we have ever had a cross word.

'You have to complement your partner, you have to make up for any weaknesses they might have. Not that Al had any! Well, there was one thing. We got badly beaten by Coventry in 1983. Terry Gibson, a tricky little striker, got a hat-trick and so every now and then, the staff, probably Ronnie Moran, would say to me, "Terry Gibson". Al's legs were so long and little figures might get in around him. They had this theory that Al's only (slight) weakness might be smaller lads. I'd be leaving a dressing room and one of them would just whisper, "Terry Gibson". But it was the same with me and Nealy to my left. If we were facing a quick left winger, they'd say to me, "Half a pace to the right," meaning, just be aware of Nealy. Not quick Phil, but what a footballer! I'm sure things were whispered about my game but it was all for the team and the thing is Alan and I never fell out. We'd just play. No big plan. If we made a mistake we both had the pace to rectify it.'

Pre-dating Hansen and Lawrenson were John Wile and Ally Robertson at West Bromwich Albion, a pair that might have scholars blowing the dust off their Latin phrasebooks for the term, *'Fucking colossal'*. Wile hailed from a mining village in Durham, while Robertson was from West Lothian in Scotland. Both left their home towns and made the centre of football's defence their noble kingdoms. No cute differences here. Both giants. Both big, both strong and both the kind of units who wouldn't care to be called brave, for brave is for those smaller types of human beings.

At the Albion both men, playing behind the spellbinding brilliance on offer from the likes of Cyrille Regis and Laurie Cunningham, offered stability – they offered reassurance. Television presenter Adrian Chiles was taken to The Hawthornes from the age of six by his grandfather, and the day offered the boy a wonderful routine. 'I'd play a school match in the morning, and my grandad would pick me up about midday,' Chiles says. 'We'd drive to the Albion the back way, there was a fish n' chip shop we'd always go to. He'd go in, and he'd buy chicken and chips, open, with curry sauce poured all over the top. We'd get to the ground and he'd leave me in the car and he'd go into the supporters' club for a couple of pints with his mates. I'd sit and watch the car park slowly fill up as I listened to the match build up on the radio, I'd do my homework, eat my chips, and get nervous for the game.

'Then at quarter to three, he'd take me into the ground and we'd sit next to the same people. I'd get a Glacier Mint when we arrived and even now if I have one, I'm back there at that time, and what I can see are these two centre-halves, as much a part of my childhood routine as the chips or those mints. Wile and Robertson, always there, the anchors of the whole thing, and you couldn't imagine it working without the two of them there. They were a fixture in all our lives. You felt love and excitement for the great attackers we had back then, but with Wile and Robertson there was respect. Absolute respect. It was different to adulation. They were the supervisors of the team.'

Talking to these centre-halves about their partnerships, long forged friendships are never far from the surface. Like old cops who used to walk a beat with each other, ready to help each other, ready to pass on knowledge and experience. Frank Leboeuf welcomed Marcel Desailly to Chelsea in the summer of 1998, just weeks after both won the World Cup with France. 'We had a good understanding,' says Leboeuf. 'We knew how to work with each other. He could also benefit from my experiences in England. Marcel made his debut at Coventry, I think, and I said, "Be careful, they don't respect reputations here." Marcel, a big man, shrugged it off. The first few minutes, Dion Dublin crashed into him and sent him over the advertising hoardings, and I said,

"I told you." From there he learnt and could handle most of them. He was a rock.'

Or you can just make a bit of money from them. 'Yeah, I was happy Marcel was with us. He helped double my wage!' laughs Leboeuf. 'He was on four times my salary, so I went to Colin Hutchinson, Chelsea's chief executive, and said, "Hey, Colin, I am also a champion of the world." He said, "How much do you want?" and I said, "Double it."

'"OK," he replied.

'Thanks, partner.'

EPILOGUE

One generation of England footballers, laden with carrying the public perception of gold, used to start training in small groups, working in marked boxes on their touch. In one box you would find the squad's regulars. The elite. Those with a touch of that gold. Paul Scholes, Frank Lampard, Wayne Rooney. Players who make things happen. Among them though is Rio Ferdinand. A centre-half. A player paid to make things stop. But such was his ability on the ball, Ferdinand was a proud member of a group he himself nicknamed 'Coutts', while those working elsewhere he labelled 'Barclays'.

Aside from giving us a clue about top footballers' banking habits, this is a reminder of the genuine oak-panelled quality England has possessed at centre-half over the years, a reminder that perceptions of the big brute too many onlookers too often take them for must be questioned, and hopefully this book has gone some way towards challenging them.

Having said that, the great big British centre-half should be celebrated in all their guises. British football still has an identity of its own. Yes, it is touched and blessed by hands from overseas but it retains something uniquely brutish. Pep Guardiola himself was struck by the importance of the 'second ball', when he arrived, that rush to get stuck in. German centre-half, Per

Mertesacker, was taken by how an English crowd would cheer a hard tackle, even if the ball is robustly put into the stand.

The Spanish football journalist Guillem Balagué admitted, without naming names, that plenty of strikers from his country had confided in him over the years to say that they enjoyed coming to play in England, where the centre-halves are slow in thought and in movement, unable to deal with gazelle-like motions and thoughts, seeing their new home as a place where goals are easier to come by.

So thoughts and perceptions will remain about the British game, and within that, the British centre-half, but what can't be disputed is their great contribution to the game. Far from simply 'stoppers', these are footballers who contribute. And yes, a Bobby Moore tackle timed as if a Swiss watchmaker had had a say can lift the soul, but so too can a tackle that shakes that soul, a towering header that sends the ball back to its maker, a slalom run with the ball from one half to another that belies a player's place in the game, or a call to arms from a leader who'd make Wellington blush.

They've come in all shapes and sizes. Been asked to do all sorts of things. Play in all sorts of formations. Stop, sweep, start. Play, kick, fight. Football's centre-half has travelled the trajectory of the sport's history with fascinating fluidity. Has any other position in the game evolved so much? Has any other position been more consistently asked to reinvent itself?

From the Edwardian playmaker to the pragmatic pre-war stopper, to the sweeper, to the *libero*, to the bruising, battle-hardened clogger, the modern everyman, our centre-half is a microcosm of the game itself. Like football, they are always changing, they are different things to different cultures, they are hard but skilful, thuggish but poetic.

Virgil van Dijk is the perfect example of both the physical and the erudite delights at the position he plays. 'I think being a centre-half at one of the biggest clubs in the world is a delight,' he says with a smile. 'I enjoy every bit of it. Being important for the team, being very vocal, organising a great side: it's fantastic. I am involved in everything. A lot of the time I have the ball, and you know, it is so nice to be the face of the modern-day centre-half. People look up to us now. The game has evolved and it is just nice that we can show a different side.'

The future shows no sign of halting that evolution. The game is changing. Topics such as the dangers of heading the ball and today's demand for technical, concise footwork in and around the narrow confines of the centre-half's penalty box (and they do think it's theirs) has created cerebral players who must keep a focus throughout a game, but as we have seen the game never sits still and while the big man heading a heavy ball back into the clouds will surely never be reinstated amid those very real concerns regarding a player's health, tactics will change again and the more physical 'battle' between centre-half and centre-forward fighting to meet a winger's inviting cross can be reasonably expected to one day return.

Young centre-halves wouldn't complain. We have seen that it is their DNA to mark not only forwards but their territory. We have read in these pages that keeping their goal safe is what they put their boots on for. Yes, there must be an element of team play, and yes, they certainly have the talent to do that, but prowling about their space, and growling at those in different colours, who might seek to enter that domain is and will remain second nature. It has to. Goals cannot come easy, there must be mountains to climb and while those forwards who scale them are forever lauded, the mountains themselves are equally as beautiful.

Football people will have their own images, their own thoughts about what makes a great centre-half. Should they be bloodied like Terry Butcher or unruffled like Alan Hansen? Should their faces be broken like Steve Bruce or immaculate like Virgil van Dijk? Should they pass the ball like Gerard Piqué or tackle like John Terry? They can in fact be everything, and they are.

Close your eyes and think of a spring afternoon at Arsenal's old Highbury stadium in 1998. A ground that first housed the withdrawn stopper centre-half in the late 1920s is now witness to one centre-half, Steve Bould, delicately lifting the ball over an opposing defence for his on-rushing partner Tony Adams to put the ball under his spell before ordering it into the net with a pulsating left-foot shot.

Not only did that goal help seal a league title, it ignited those constantly changing thoughts about the centre-half. They must play the game in so many different ways, with so many different expectations. They are and always will be football's enigmas. Today they are celebrated for their all-round play, but when interviewed for these pages, Kenny Burns, Nottingham Forest's centre-half in their 1970s glory days, was asked what he thought about the modern master, Virgil van Dijk.

'I don't like him,' came the curt reply.

'Why not?'

'He's too skilful.'

When it comes to centre-halves, some things may never change.

ACKNOWLEDGEMENTS

It started as an embryonic idea in my mud-soaked head as I struggled to cling onto my fading youth on the pitches of Hackney Marshes one cold Sunday morning. There, playing at centre-half (onlookers might argue I was more Frank Spencer than Franco Baresi) I began to wonder about a book on the position that had always interested me. Why not? Football might be the beautiful game, but that beauty can be found in less obvious places.

For taking my idea and making it a reality, I want to first thank Matthew Lowing at Bloomsbury. From a first meeting over a coffee some time ago, he has been a constant champion of our book: organising, encouraging and chest-beating like any great central defender. I'd also like to thank Zoë Blanc at Bloomsbury for her brilliant editing skills. Thank you to James Watson at Bloomsbury for the cover design, and to Austin Taylor for designing the plate section.

To all the many footballers, past and present who contributed to these pages, thank you for your time and enthusiasm. A special thank you to Patrick Barclay, Guillem Balague, Sam Pilger, Duncan Ross, Henry Winter, Pat Murphy, Jeff Whitely, Adrian Chiles, Mark Lawrenson, Ian Ridley, Jonny Owen, Kevin Taylor, Philippe Auclair, Harry Redknapp, Archie Macpherson, Alan Reeves, Tom Craig, Glenn McNamara, David Luxton, Mark Riches, my beautiful mum Clare Moynihan, Leroy Rosenior, and finally thank you to Melanie Orban for almost becoming interested in centre-halves.

BIBLIOGRAPHY

Adams, T. & Ridley, I. (2017) *Addicted* (London: HarperCollins)
— (2018) *Sober: Football. My Story. My Life.* (London: Simon & Schuster)
Barclay, P. (2015) *The Life and Times of Herbert Chapman: The Story of One of Football's Most Influential Figures* (London: Weidenfeld & Nicolson)
— (2017) *Sir Matt Busby: The Definitive Biography* (London: Ebury)
Butcher, T. (2005) *Butcher: My Autobiography* (Lewes: Highdown)
Butler, B. & Greenwood, R. (1979) *Soccer Choice* (London: Pelham Books)
Campomar, A. (2014) *¡Golazo!: A History of Latin American* Football (London: Quercus)
Charlton, J. (1997) *Jack Charlton: The Autobiography* (London: Corgi)
Cox, M. (2017) *The Mixer* (London: Harper Collins)
Ferguson, A. (2000) *Managing My Life* (London: Hodder and Stoughton)
— (2013) *My Autobiography* (London: Hodder and Stoughton)
Giller, N. (2002*) Billy Wright: A Hero for All Seasons* (London: Robson Books)
Glanville, B. (1955) *Soccer Nemesis* (London: Secker & Warburg)
Green, G. (1953) *Soccer: The World Game: A Popular History* (London: Pelham Books)
Hansen, A. (2010) *A Matter of Opinion* (London: Bantam)
Holden, J. (2013) *Stan Cullis: The Iron Manager* (Nottingham: DB Publishing)
Kuper, S. (1994) *Football Against the Enemy* (London: Orion)
Ledbrooke, A. & Turner, E. (1950) *Soccer from the Press Box* (London: Nicholas Kave)
Macpherson, A. (2014) *Jock Stein: The Definitive Biography* (London: Racing Post Books)
Mertesacker, P. (2019) *Big Friendly German* (Liverpool: deCoubertin Books)
Moynihan, J. (1968) *The Soccer Syndrome* (London: Sportsmans Book Club)
Powell, J. (1993) *Bobby Moore* (London: Robson Books)
Thomas, J. & Shilton, P. (1982) *The Magnificent Obsession* (Worthing: Littlehampton Book Services Ltd.)
Thompson, P. (1996) *Do That Again Son and I'll Break Your Legs* (London: Virgin Books)
— (2006) *Emlyn Hughes: A Tribute to Crazy Horse* (Cheltenham: Stadia)
Wilson, J. (2013) *The Outsider: A History of the Goalkeeper* (London: Orion)
— *(2008) Inverting the Pyramid: The History of Football Tactics* (London: Weidenfeld & Nicolson)

INDEX